I0168741

BEFORE YOU GO TO AMERICA

BEFORE YOU GO TO AMERICA

NINE EASY LESSONS NO ONE
THOUGHT TO TELL YOU

By Olusegun Michael Abidoye

© 2020 by Olusegun Michael Abidoye

All rights reserved. This book or any portion thereof may not be repro-
duced or used in any manner whatsoever without the express written
permission of the publisher except for the use of brief quotations in a
book review.

ISBN: 978-1-7347547-1-1

Although the author and publisher have made every effort to ensure that
the information in this book was correct at press time, the author and
publisher do not assume and hereby disclaim any liability to any party for
any loss, damage, or disruption caused by errors or omissions, whether
such errors or omissions result from negligence, accident, or any other
cause.

This book is not intended as a substitute for the medical, legal, accounting or other professional services and/or advice. The reader should regu-
larly consult with medical, legal, accounting or other professional services
as needed.

DEDICATION

First of all, I give thanks to Almighty God for giving me the courage and strength to pursue this book. Also, I'm dedicating this book to my beloved mother, Abosede Abidoye (may her soul rest in perfect peace), and to my dearest father, Captain Olugbemiga Abidoye, both of whom always give me the strength needed to push forward, push harder, and never give up.

CONTENTS

FOREWORD

One poignant Nigerian proverb that is laden with advanced wisdom says: *A chicken that comes into a new territory for the first time stands on one foot.* This proverb, apparently developed from years of observing nature with keen attention, takes note of the uncommon habit of chickens to tread softly—really, first standing on one foot—when they are in unfamiliar territory. The essence of this caution is the deep philosophy that must be imbibed by every being—in particular, humans. It is an admonition to every being not to barge into new terrain full of confidence, enthusiasm, and swagger. It is a caveat that coming to new grounds demands caution and wisdom, which is precisely what the proverbial chicken is considered to be doing: exercising caution and wisdom that entail visual and mental scanning of the area, consideration of what to encounter, introspection on how to fit in with minimal friction, contemplation of the best ways to avoid conflict, and, above all, looking out for the first set of approachable folk, the first friends to make.

This is what Olusegun Michael Abidoye has most efficiently succeeded in putting across to people coming to the United

States for the first time, especially as immigrants. The title of the 168-page book crisply puts across its intention, while the subtitle unambiguously hints at the fact that the inherent advice is not always *just there* for the immigrant or intending immigrant: somebody needs to guide you right!

Before You Go to America: Nine Easy Lessons No One Thought to Tell You is a didactic, virtually DIY utility book that is presented in a most comprehensive way as a down-to-earth guide for the ever-increasing stream of young, eager, and at times desperate people, mostly from the world's growing nations, who wish to migrate to the United States for varying reasons, but mainly for self-improvement, education, and emotional and social stability. At the background of the imperativeness of this book is the fact that many an immigrant or intending immigrant is faced with a dearth of valid and sincere information, leaving many blank and at the mercy of sharks who exploit their lack of precise information. Very many "get lost" in the mire of fast-moving and impersonal life, quite divergent from where they were uprooted from, so to say. Uprooted, because quite a large percentage of immigrants would, if they had their way, have remained in their own countries to build the natural dream of the young and vibrant: to join in building a great country. Irrespective of the finances available to a young immigrant, they all must also face challenges of being on their own for the very first time, away from parental watch, peer camaraderie, and a familiar environmental cocoon.

The mere fact of the social and emotional thresholds of many immigrants makes them quite vulnerable to making errors that the impatient American system often misinterprets as deliberate crimes. This fact therefore accentuates the need for them to be well guided by information from well-intended sources like this great and fundamental work by Abidoye. The book is clear evidence of a painstaking compilation of oxygen-giving counsel not easy to find in one single location. It speaks of the innate heart of the writer, which is manifested in an altruistic desire to ensure that fewer immigrants and would-be immigrants succumb the numerous challenges of moving to "strange" lands.

In the nine chapters that make this 168 pager, virtually *everything* they would want to know is presented, and in light, free-flowing language replete with humor and mirth. Chapter 1, "The United States of America and Its way of Life," gives the reader a snappy view of the US, from the country's motto to its capital, language, ethnic groups and population ratios, religion, and currency, right down to which side of the road to drive on. It gives a wide angle view on how the people of that country live. Chapter 2, "Learn and Master Your Craft," counsels the reader on the need to focus on hard work, and, importantly, how to manage the sudden expectations of support by family and friends at "home," many of whom imagine that mere migration is in itself a gold mine. The chapter advises on how to manage oneself. Chapter 3, which treats "Your Health, Your Concern," provides essential advice on management of one's health and how to benefit from the vast array of opportunities like health insurance, access to good doctors and nurses—a network the author describes as complex. It is critical for the immigrant to understand the system.

Chapter 4 is titled "Education in the USA" and tells the reader about the school structure, the grading systems, and the heavy focus placed on STEM (science, technology, engineering, and mathematics). It is necessary for people "going to America" to keep this in mind in making study and career decisions. It makes all the difference in their well-being and their future. Chapter 5, "The American Credit System," draws attention to credit, that honey pot that could become a poisoned chalice when an immigrant gets carried away by the ostensibly alluring opportunity to buy and buy and buy. Chapter 6 deals with "Money and Wealth" and treats financial intelligence, investments, bank accounts, cash-flow, and income opportunities. This looks like the pearl chapter, because many immigrants fall short in managing their finances, often through not understanding the divergences between the American financial system and those in their home countries.

In Chapter 7, "Taxes," Abidoye gives down-to-earth advice on the intricate taxation regime, which could throw the unwitting into grave situations. This is largely because many immigrants come from countries in which paying taxes is rated low—largely due to the failure of governments to apply national revenues to the common good. The chapter acquaints the reader with the US taxation system, filing tax returns, and commonly used tax forms. Chapter 8 is titled "Immigration"—which speaks for itself. It methodologically takes immigrants and prospective immigrants through the processes of migrating legally to the US. It identifies the various initiatives and programs, from arrival/departure procedures to seeking permanent residency, to seeking the green card, to obtaining citizenship, the ultimate prize of many, if not most, immigrants from growing countries. Chapter 9 treats the "Sex Culture," a blend of the serious, the capricious, and the absurd. Liberalism. Exposure. Tolerance. Limits. Consent. LGBTQ. These issues, and more, often come as a major source of culture shock to the immigrant. In the midst of the apparently liberated atmosphere, the immigrant soon finds out that the free spirit does not mean that one can do just what one pleases—and that one can, generally speaking, not take liberties with members of the opposite gender.

In this first book of his, Abidoye has produced a master work that should have wide appeal to general audiences, especially secondary school students and graduates in growing countries, who are about to migrate or have just migrated in the span of two to three years. The book is listed among works by Amazon's Elite Authors and is rated by the Optimized Amazon Listing as good for social sciences, emigration/immigration, travel, and US and general BISAC (Book Industry Standards and Communication). It deems the book as being able to help people, especially Africans and Nigerians coming to the US, in the following critical ways: as a guide for immigrants coming to the US, showing how American people live, understanding the culture and customs, learning to think like an American, and how to move to another country.

Olusegun Michael Abidoye was born in Lagos, Nigeria, and left Nigeria at the young age of sixteen for the US. He apparently came as a serious-minded and focused young man, because he settled in for studies, and obtained a BS in Electrical Engineering in 2005 from Bradley University in Peoria, Illinois. He obtained an MS also in Electrical Engineering, specializing in Controls and Embedded Systems. He has thereafter had quite a rich professional career, including being a senior manager, project manager, automation and controls engineer, and electrical manager in *Fortune 100* companies, including Nestlé, agriculture and biofuels giant Archer Daniels Midland (ADM), and Crown Cork and Seal. His project management portfolio has over the years ranged up to a sizeable $25 million.

It is not all work for Abidoye. He has a good range of leisure interests that include soccer, movies, traveling, lounge and jazz clubs, cooking, nature, and landscape photography. All of these generate in Abidoye a perfect mix of a man and a lucid mind that is eloquent in the meticulous output that is this work. In *Before You Go to America,* Abidoye has shown the pluck of a caring persona, eager to show the mentoring ropes to fresh immigrants. Indeed, this book should be a *vade mecum* for everyone living in the United States.

He has done great service to the immigrant population of the US and all other countries to which people migrate. He has done a good turn to droves of young persons from growing countries who are keen (rightly or wrongly) to migrate to the US. He has done justice to misconceptions and prejudices that exist in American society about people coming in from other countries. Above all, he has done well for himself as a start-up serious author and a worthy ambassador of good causes.

Josef Bel-Molokwu, PhD
beljosef2@gmail.com

Senior Fellow at the School of Media and Communication, Pan-Atlantic University, Lagos, Nigeria. Communication and Media Consultant. Fellow in Intercontinental Communication. Fellow in Management Consultancy. Fellow of Advertising. Past chief executive of the Advertising Practitioners Council of Nigeria. Past editor/editor-in-chief/editorial adviser. Past CEO of three newspaper houses.

August 22, 2020

PREFACE

You must be wondering why on earth someone would write a book or a compilation of simple one-page lessons about the most marketed, most diversified, most powerful country in the world. Well, let's just say this is a book I wished I had been given when I first came to the shores of the United States of America. This is a book that would have helped me avoid some common mistakes and pitfalls that could easily have been avoided with a little information or perhaps education.

This is a book I have written to my younger self—to learn quickly and hit the ground not even running, but walking. It is a book that does not attempt to answer all your questions. However, it is written with this objective in mind: for you to start to know where to look and what questions to ask, and to stimulate your thoughts in the right direction as you begin your journey here in the United States, in the land of opportunity.

Before You Go to America is written in a manner to be most effective: as one-point lessons with each topic page attempts to convey one lesson all by itself.

I hope that with this book, some of you will learn and leverage the lessons that no one else will tell you, and that you will learn from simple mistakes and pitfalls that certainly can be avoided. This book will help to broaden your horizons in what I believe to be very important subjects that you, the chief executive of your own life, need to manage to find success.

I wish you the best and good luck to you. This is a long-haul journey; buckle up!

CHAPTER 1

The United States of America and Its Way of Life

Intro and quick facts

- Motto: "In God we Trust"
- Capital: Washington, DC
- Largest city: New York City
- National language: English
- Ethnic groups: 77 percent white, 13 percent Black, 6 percent Asian, 3 percent multiracial, 1 percent Native American, 0.2 percent Pacific Islander.
- Ethnic groups ethnicity: 18 percent Hispanic or Latino, 82 percent non-Hispanic or non-Latino
- Religion: 73 percent Christian, 21 percent unaffiliated, 2 percent Jewish, 1 percent Muslim, 3 percent other
- Population: 327 million (2018 estimate)
- Currency: United States dollars (USD, $)
- Driving side: Right side

Government and political parties

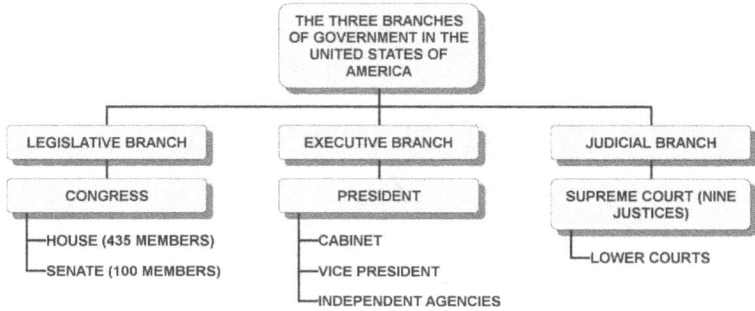

```
                    THE THREE BRANCHES
                    OF GOVERNMENT IN THE
                    UNITED STATES OF
                    AMERICA

   LEGISLATIVE BRANCH      EXECUTIVE BRANCH        JUDICIAL BRANCH

      CONGRESS                PRESIDENT         SUPREME COURT (NINE
                                                     JUSTICES)

  HOUSE (435 MEMBERS)      CABINET
  SENATE (100 MEMBERS)     VICE PRESIDENT          LOWER COURTS
                           INDEPENDENT AGENCIES
```

It is important to know that all the three branches of government are coequal, and they do the following:

10. **The legislative branch** makes the law.
11. **The executive branch** executes the law.
12. **The judicial branch** interprets the law.

The major political parties that have dominated American politics are the following:

1. The Democratic Party—center-left liberal party.
2. The Republican Party (a.k.a. the GOP, Grand Old Party)—center-right conservative party.

Other parties include

1. The Libertarian Party
2. The Green Party
3. The Constitution Party

What is culture shock—will it get to you?

Culture shock is commonly referred to as an experience a person may have when he or she moves to a different cultural environment. It can result in disorientation when experiencing an unfamiliar way abroad.

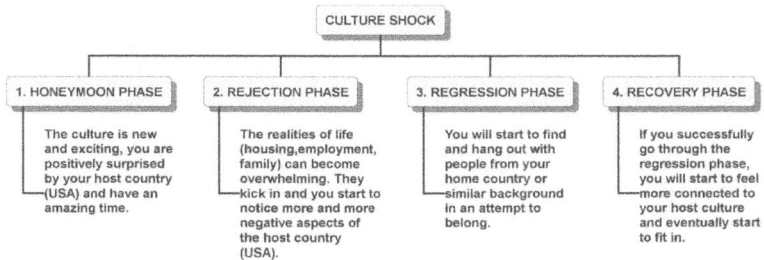

CULTURE SHOCK

1. HONEYMOON PHASE	2. REJECTION PHASE	3. REGRESSION PHASE	4. RECOVERY PHASE
The culture is new and exciting, you are positively surprised by your host country (USA) and have an amazing time.	The realities of life (housing,employment, family) can become overwhelming. They kick in and you start to notice more and more negative aspects of the host country (USA).	You will start to find and hang out with people from your home country or similar background in an attempt to belong.	If you successfully go through the regression phase, you will start to feel more connected to your host culture and eventually start to fit in.

From the website http://www.aiesec.nl, from which the chart above is taken, you will most likely go through these four phases as you experience culture shock: the honeymoon phase, the rejection phase, the regression phase, and, lastly, the recovery phase. I want to point out to you to take heart. You will eventually move to the recovery phase, and these things take time. Do not pack your bags and go back home from where you came.

So, when I arrived the United States (like most of you reading this now can relate to), I was very excited to be here. This is a country that, for so long, has been talked about only in the best of terms. This is a country with many opportunities, where you can be whatever you want to be and do whatever you want to do. The freedom that comes with it—well, let's just say I was superglad, superexcited when the plane took off from Lagos

Nigeria Murtala Mohammed Airport. My mother always told me never to fully believe I was leaving Nigeria until the plane left the runway and took off, and even then, to keep my fingers crossed that the plane didn't return to Nigeria. But we landed at John F. Kennedy airport in New York.

Can you imagine that after all the euphoric feelings (well, I bet you can!), I was ready to pack my bags and return home, back to Lagos? So, first of all, there was nothing I enjoyed eating. Everything tasted funny and felt foreign; it was cold and getting colder; even the Coke and Pepsi tasted very different here, and I didn't like it. The peak of my frustration was when I got sick and didn't know where to turn to for help. I was so sick that I couldn't make it to class for four days. It was too cold for me to get any medications. I didn't really know too many people whom I could trust (much less feel comfortable with). I was completely and utterly miserable. I stayed in my room, in my bed, for the whole four days, under my comforter. I survived on cookies, water, and the occasional Coke I would swirl in my mouth, only to conclude again it was not the real Coke. I didn't even know what medications to get once I managed to get out of my room.

You see the whole theme here: confusion, frustration, and the readiness to go back home to my father, mother, sisters, brother, and friends—all who love me, all who know my name.

If you have seen the show *Friends*, you would better understand my joke reference here: when Joey traveled to London for Ross's wedding, and he felt homesick. He wanted to go back home to America where people knew his name…ha! This was how I felt. I was done, ready to go home. My friend Babatunde helped me get through this. I went from the honeymoon phase to the rejection phase in a span of less than six months. I must say that in the next couple of years, I experienced different cycles of culture shock, each different, each revealing of my new environment.

Oh, by the way: WELCOME TO AMERICA!

Culture shock—symptoms

Below are some typical symptoms of culture shock, so you can recognize them early on. Recognition is the first step to effectively combating it.

- Sadness, loneliness, melancholy
- Preoccupation with health
- Aches, pains, allergies
- Insomnia or excessive sleep
- Changes in mood
- Anger, irritability
- Lack of confidence
- Longing for family
- Feelings of being lost or overlooked

From my personal experience, cheer up, I would say. Looking back now over nineteen years, I understand now that while I felt these things, I didn't realize them until many years later. These are not permanent, and they will surely pass as you move forward with your integration into American society. This is what I aim to help you prepare for.

Combating culture shock—what you should do

In your first two weeks in America, do this:

1. Get a mobile phone. Choose any of the following options:
   a. Use an unlocked phone from home. Purchase a new sim card in the USA.
   b. Buy new phone. Set up a prepaid plan.
   c. Buy a new cell phone. Set up a contract plan.
2. Fight your desire to sleep during daylight.
3. Open a bank account and set up debit and/or credit cards.
4. Order bank checks, register online for internet banking, and download their mobile applications to your phone.

Generally, according to internationalstudent.com, you should do the following:

- Remind yourself that this feeling is normal.
- Connect and keep in touch with family and friends back home.
- Have pictures and reminders of home. These will come in handy.
- Eat healthy and balanced meals.
- Find food you are familiar with.
- Find your faith or religious communities, your ethnic group, or fellow countrymen.

- Maintain your confidence in yourself and follow the ambitions and plans that brought you here to America in the first place.
- Lastly, practice having VFCD (vision, focus, commitment, and dedication)!

American culture and values

Folks, look: the bottom line is that American culture is very different; it's not like anything you are used to. There are many different groups, communities, and locations, all with their own uniqueness. However, they all share and embody some key values. These are:

1. **Independence**: In America, you are your own person and have control of your own life and all the choices and decisions that affect it.

2. **Equality**: The American Declaration of Independence states, "All men are created equal." Americans believe everyone is equal and that everyone is free.

3. **Informality**: Americans tend to be informal in dress, speech, and posture. Everyone is on a first-name basis. Do not mistake this for rudeness. It is how things are done here.

4. **Directness**: Frankness and openness—these are treasured in America. If you have a problem, concern, or issue, speak up. Be clear and direct in order to come up with a viable solution that is robust enough and cares for all the different parties.

Some US holidays and customs to know

Date/Day	Info	Description
January 1	New Year's Day	America loves to have parties the night before.
3rd Monday in January	Martin Luther King Jr. Day	MLK, one of America's greatest civil right leaders, is commemorated.
February 14	Valentine's Day	This is a day of love, romance, chocolates, flowers, and gifts for your special someone.
Third Monday of February	Presidents' Day	The US honors past presidents.
March 17	St. Patrick's Day	The US celebrates the patron saint of Ireland with parades, parties, and everything green—including green beer!
April 1	April Fool's Day	This is the day to play a harmless, clever trick on your friends and loved ones.
Last Monday of May	Memorial Day	The men and women who served and died in the US armed forces are remembered.
July 4	Independence Day	Americans celebrate the day the United States declared independence from England.
First Monday in September	Labor Day	American workers are celebrated throughout the country.
Second Monday in October	Columbus Day	This day is a tribute to Christopher Columbus, who is thought of as the discoverer of the Americas.

Last Thursday in November	Thanksgiving Day	Celebrate the dinner shared by the first settlers in America with Native Americans. A turkey is usually the main food attraction.
December 25	Christmas Day	Celebrate the birth of Christ.

Social life

From my limited experience, social life in the United States of America is completely yours to initiate and develop in whatever way you can sustain and are comfortable with.

Remember, Americans are very nice and polite; they will ask you very simple questions. If deeper relationships are to evolve, it is up to you, period!

- Be assertive.
- Invite people out for coffee or drinks.
- Work out and exercise with friends.
- Have people over to your home, and learn about each other.
- Give it time, and be open to new things.
- Don't be pushy.

It is worth mentioning that the United States has a big tipping culture for their service-and-hospitality industry. For example, when you go to a restaurant for lunch or dinner, grab a coffee, or even take a taxi to a destination, you are expected to tip your host. Tips range anywhere from 15 percent to 25 percent of the total cost of service, depending on your group size. Tips are necessary as supplemental income for those in these industries, as sometimes they earn the bare minimum wage possible, and their employers expect them to make up the difference via the tips that they collect.

America is a very big country that enjoys a diverse range of activities, including outdoor activities such as cookouts, sailing, and camping. They are big on coffee, tea, beers, and wines. Be positive, know and manage yourself and your relationships, and nurture and grow them.

Accommodations

You are a new resident here in America, and your choices of housing are quite extensive. I have taken the liberty of mentioning the most common three options and including some quick notes on them. Note that these are just to give you some ideas and to stimulate your thoughts so you can start to ask the right questions and seek the answers you deserve.

Accommodation	Quick Notes
Staying with a relative	If you are fortunate enough to have family here in the United States, be mindful that your presence, especially long term, will increase the overall household expense, *so pitch in, any way you can!*
Leasing an apartment	Using Chicago (where I currently live) as an example, rent for a studio is about $1,000 to $1,200 per month. You will need to have the first month's rent, plus a security deposit, which is usually equal to one month's rent. This is usually refundable at the end of the lease agreement. You might need a cosigner if you don't have any credit history. Do not forget to ask about utilities and who or what party is responsible for them. You have typically electric, gas, and water.

Buying a home	If you are fortunate enough to fall in the category where you can afford to buy your home, this note is just a brief highlight of what you will need.

- A down payment of 3.5 percent–5 percent of the purchase price.
- An amount equal to 3.5 percent–5 percent of purchase price for closing costs, things like legal, appraisals, taxes, and so on.
- You might need a cosigner if you do not have good enough credit.

Transportation

- Bicycles: You can rent or buy one—very convenient in city centers.
- Buses: This would require tickets to be purchased or pay a fare as you get on the bus.
- Taxis: Schedule one via a phone call or flag one down on the streets. It's usually very convenient in busy centers.
- Ride-sharing services (Uber/Lyft): Get their mobile applications.
- Trains: This would require tickets to be purchased.
- Purchase a car: You would need a 3 percent–5 percent down payment and maybe a cosigner if you do not have credit. You would need insurance.

Money—United States currency

United States currency is a decimal-based system: 1 USD (one dollar) = $1.00, equal to one hundred cents.

Coins are for amounts less than one dollar. The most popular are the following:

- **Penny** = one cent, or 0.01 dollars
- **Nickel** = five cents, or 0.05 dollars
- **Dime** = ten cents, or 0.10 dollars
- **Quarter** = twenty-five cents, or 0.25 dollars

Be patient with yourself as you learn this new currency, the denominations, and the power behind the dollar.

Paper currency is printed in white and green in the following denominations:

- **$1** = one dollar
- **$5** = five dollars
- **$10** = ten dollars
- **$20** = twenty dollars
- **$50** = fifty dollars
- **$100** = one hundred dollars.

Why is it important to know the denominations and US currency? Well, let's just say I gave away a twenty-dollar bill to someone I met outside the local pharmacy asking everyone that came out for cash. In my mind, using a conversion rate of the Nigerian naira at the time, this was acceptable; however, I just forgot to add an extra zero in the calculations done in my head. What I meant to give was two dollars.

Bank Accounts

One of the first things you'll need to do is open a bank account. Later I will describe in more details how to structure this, but for now, to open a bank account, you will need the following:

1. A current passport or government-issued ID.
2. Proof of address—a utility bill with your name or a piece of mail.
3. A personal ID number such as
   a. A Social Security number;
   b. A passport number;
   c. An international ID number with photo; or
   d. An individual taxpayer number.

Note that Social Security numbers are not issued automatically. You must have been in the United States for at least ten days and be authorized to work. One can be obtained by applying in a Social Security Administration office.

Ask about and familiarize yourself with all fees associated with the type of account you are opening with the bank or financial institution, any deposit or withdrawal restrictions, and/or any penalties.

Daylight saving time

Daylight saving time in America is a bittersweet experience that will make most of you wonder exactly what is going on. And if you are like me, you'll think you've achieved something great. So let's start by saying that daylight saving time is the act, in most of the United States, of changing the time either forward or backward by one hour. In the fall, the clock is moved backward, and in the spring, the clock is moved forward. What does this mean? Let's say the time is 3:00 a.m. In the spring, on the second Sunday of March, when daylight saving time begins, the clock is moved forward to 4:00 a.m., so you lose an hour. On the first Sunday in November, when daylight saving time ends, the clock is moved back to 2:00 a.m. You gain an extra hour.

So remember: "Fall backward; spring forward." This is the most popular way of remembering exactly what is going on.

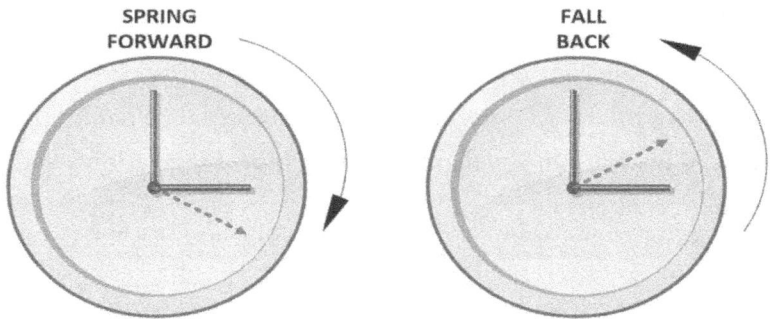

Why would an entire country do this? you may ask. Why would any country feel the need to change the clock? Who gave them that power? Very good question. Honestly, I was just as shocked the very first time this happened to me as you are now reading about it. The whole thing is done so that the evenings have more daylight and the mornings have less daylight. For example, here in Chicago, in the winter months, sunsets start as early as 5:00 p.m. And in the summer months, the sunset typically could start as late as 8:00 p.m. The clock is changed to move the day by one hour, so we get to play more in the sun—or, rather, more responsibly, do more business in the day.

The very first time I experienced this was in college. Usually my calculus I class was at 9:00 a.m. in the fall semester, and because no one ever bothered to tell me anything, I showed up for class at 9:00 a.m., which, by the way, had been changed backward to 8:00 a.m. I was super excited and felt good, and proud of myself, thinking that I was the first person in the class. After about twenty minutes of waiting in a classroom that was still very much empty, I thought that the professor had canceled the class and I had just missed the email, since I didn't have a phone, let alone a smartphone. These were the days when I had to go to the library to check email on the shared computers. So I went back to my room and resumed what I had been doing before, which was get under my bedcovers and sleep, until my next class, at 1:00 p.m. A friend of mine walked into my room and asked, "Why didn't you show up for class?" I felt so stupid after he explained the whole thing to me.

So please know that this is something that is done twice each year here in the United States. Don't be caught waiting for a bus on the wrong time schedule or standing for a train to arrive on a cold winter morning at the wrong time. It is fun. You gain, as I like to put it, an extra hour of sleep in the fall, but then you have to give this time back in the spring. Like everything else here in this book, ask more questions, do your own independent research, and expand your breadth of knowledge on these topics.

CHAPTER 2

Learn and Master Your Craft

Introduction

Like me, I imagine you are going to (or maybe are already in) the United States of America because you believe it will offer more prosperity to you and/or your family.

My take on this is truly simple: you get what you put in, and if you work hard and have some exceptional luck, you will go very far in America. Before you all crucify me, let us agree that luck is defined as preparation meeting opportunity.

A few notes worth mentioning:

1. Money doesn't grow on trees in America.
2. As individualistic as America is, you need every good person around you who is willing to share—not to share their fish, but their knowledge of how to fish.
3. Do not be afraid to pay for knowledge. This is the best gift you can give yourself. Never stop learning.

4. Your time is your most valuable asset. Know this and understand it.

5. Be the chief architect of your future plans. Document both short-term and long-term goals.

6. Develop a system to hold yourself accountable for what you have set yourself to do or accomplish. This system must also have a feedback loop so you can improve it and thereby improve yourself. You must use this system.

7. Lastly, I would advise that you must give back. There are many ways you can do that, be it volunteering, mentoring, making charitable donations, and so on.

You are here to win—part I

You must have heard the saying "All work and no play makes Jack a dull boy." Or maybe you have heard "Work hard and play hard." These sayings advocate for the concept of a more balanced life approach.

I am here to tell you to throw all that nonsense away. While you are in America, during your first few years, sayings like "A champion never quits" and "Champions do not know balance or moderation" are what you would want to embody.

You are here (or are about to be) in America so you can be a champion for your life, a champion for your family and loved ones. Take whatever you do very seriously, and understand its impact on your life both in the short term and, ultimately, the long term. I'll use a personal story to explain this better in part II.

A few more quotes, so this sinks into your head:

1. "Winning isn't everything; it's the only thing." (Vince Lombardi)

2. "Winning takes precedence over all. There's no gray area. No almost." (Kobe Bryant)

3. "The secret to wining is constant, consistent management." (Tom Landry)

4. Wining isn't something that you wake up and go into without a plan. Whatever grand plan you have starts with a single step, and every step you take must fit into the whole bigger picture for yourself, as you see yourself. You must learn to look at the plan in totality.

Sometimes you will lose the small battles, but your goal must be to win the war.

You are here to win...*so start winning!*

You are here to win—part II

I want to share with you my personal experience, and hopefully you will learn from it. I came to America as a young boy to study electrical engineering with a computer option. I was very happy to be in the program and in America. In my first year, I was in a very difficult class, Calculus I, taught by an American professor with a Chinese heritage. My professor's English was not the best, and I had a hard time understanding him, as if calculus weren't hard enough.

It was so difficult to comprehend that I decided to drop the class, which ultimately meant I would have to drop out of the engineering program. Calculus I was the first of four classes mandatory for engineering, to satisfy the requirements of advanced mathematics before the even harder classes in the core program could be taken.

My very good friend at the time, who also was my mentor, from the same hometown I came from, Babatunde, pulled me aside and said, "My dear brother, if I hear anything remotely close to you dropping out of any class—let's not mention engineering—I'll give you a knock on your head." This was funny at the time. However, because this was a man whom I had a great deal of respect for, he was able to influence my decision. So yes, I stayed in the program and didn't drop out.

In my third year, called the junior year, I was failing at a programming class. At the invitation of my professor, Professor Gutcshlag, I stayed behind for the winter break, and he taught me the foundational skills I lacked to comprehend the material he was teaching. I was very successful afterward and completed many similar projects.

The point is that failure was imminent; however, with the good people around me, and with hard work, resilience, and ultimately some luck, I succeeded.

My formula for winning—persevere, show grit, and win!

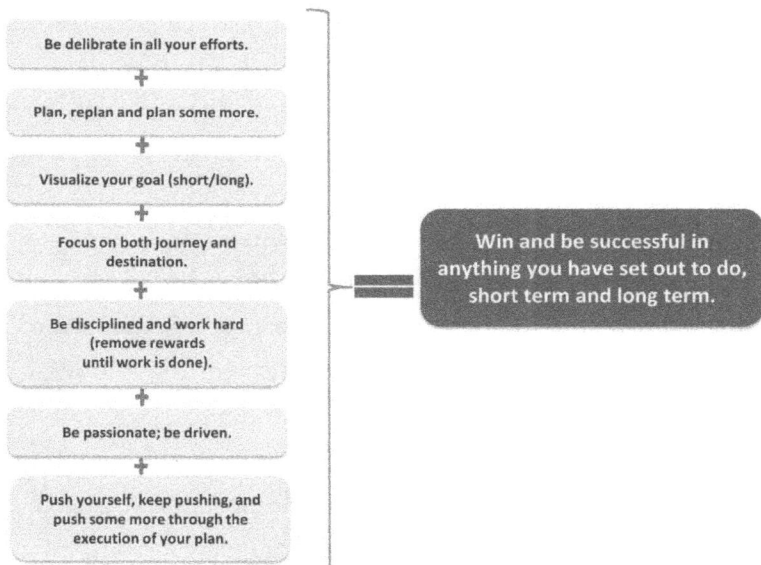

Be delibrate in all your efforts.

Plan, replan and plan some more.

Visualize your goal (short/long).

Focus on both journey and destination.

Be disciplined and work hard (remove rewards until work is done).

Be passionate; be driven.

Push yourself, keep pushing, and push some more through the execution of your plan.

Win and be successful in anything you have set out to do, short term and long term.

The chart above is what I would like to call the formula to winning. I wish I had known this formula many years ago, as opposed to just winging things. Use the formula in your system; apply it in the routine of your longer-term plans and goals.

Invest in yourself early; don't hesitate

One of the things you will need to understand is that there are several ways to invest—several types of investment vehicles and instruments. All investments carry some degree of risk.

However, the one investment that guarantees returns, that carries only the risk you personally allow or invite, is the investment in you. If you invest in yourself, you cannot go wrong. If you continue to invest in yourself, you will win!

This might seem like a mundane point of discussion; however, you will need to know this so you can apply it later on. You will come to or arrive at several initiatives and/or questions, all centered on money and the financial world.

What you should know is, if something buys you knowledge and permits personal growth and development, and then it is worth it. Below are some ideas for you to invest in yourself:

- Undergraduate degrees (associate and bachelor's degrees).
- Postgraduate studies, such as your master's degree or an MBA program.
- Fees for professional certifications—that is, human resources, PMP project management, and so on.
- Study abroad or exchange programs.
- Buying books to read (paperback, electronic, or audio).
- Fees for consultation with subject-matter experts.
- Broker fees for managing the right deals such as real estate.

- Broker fees for stock selections so you know where to put your money

There are many more. The above list is by no means exhaustive.

Start early, have no regrets, and continue to invest in yourself.

Learn how to improve yourself first

Improve yourself before you attempt to improve others. Your extended presence in America will reveal to you many truths, many aspects of the culture and the environment here in the United States.

Below is a picture showing you what you need to do to improve yourself at the core. Confront your fears, cultivate and nurture meaningful relationships that you also add value to, read a lot, invest some money in your future, don't pay attention to disturbances, be disciplined, choose what you want to achieve—only one thing—and understand the reasons why you are doing what it is you are doing. These are the ways in which you start to strengthen your core self.

You matter, and your core matters. Self-improvement and its continuous process will let you go the distance.

This is a long-term game, so pace yourself, and come prepared.

CHAPTER 3

Your Health, Your Concern!

Know your details—part I

It is very important for you to know that in the United States, one of the things that can cripple an individual and sometimes families is the rising costs of health care in the country.

This topic aims to bring your attention to the fact that the more information you can provide the health-care professionals, nurses, and doctors helping to manage your health, the better these health-care professionals can help you. You must know your specific information, and it is beneficial to monitor key metrics for your health and understand their trends, trajectories, and respective interpretations.

Your first assessment, whether it is a basic blood panel or a comprehensive blood panel, will always be your baseline. In addition, it is vital to have information readily available in the event of emergencies. I personally use the Medical ID feature on my iPhone and store details like the following:

- Blood type
- Allergies
- Weight
- Height
- Emergency contacts

Even if my iPhone is locked, this information is readily accessible by anyone should I find myself in an emergency situation. *Know your details; it could save your life.*

Know your details—part II

I want to use this opportunity to share with you what else I keep track of on either a quarterly, semiannual, or annual basis.

- Blood pressure
- Height
- Weight
- BMI (body mass index, a ratio of height to weight)
- Total cholesterol (LDL, HDL, and other lipids)
- Triglyceride (fats in the blood and body from food eaten)
- HDL (high-density lipoprotein—healthy cholesterol)
- LDL (low-density lipoprotein—bad cholesterol)
- Risk ratio (ratio of total cholesterol to HDL—indicates risk of heart disease)
- HbA1c (gives an idea about blood-sugar levels on average)
- PSA (prostate—I just started this a few years ago).

I personally monitor and track these and a few other things, and I have data over several years. With this data and information, I am able to adjust my food, diet, and exercise, and also understand myself better. This gives me better control.

I do, at the very least, an annual physical, covered through my employer-sponsored insurance:

- Blood (cholesterols, sugar levels)
- Kidney and liver functions
- Vitamins

Get your health insurance ASAP

The bottom line here is that if you do not have health insurance in America, you will be responsible for the entire cost of health care out of pocket. The United States has one of the highest (if not *the* highest, it seems sometimes) costs of medical care in the developed nations. Having health-care insurance is crucial to your survival; otherwise, do not plan on getting sick. But if you are like me, who sometimes does need the intervention of health-care professionals, get insurance as soon as you can. From www.usa.gov, here are some avenues I want you to look into pertaining to health-care coverage:

- A group coverage plan at your job or your spouse's job, if you are fortunate enough to have a job that offers employer-sponsored insurance.
- Your parents' insurance plan if you are under twenty-six years old (might not be practical for you if you just settled into the country).
- A plan you purchase on your own directly from health-insurance companies or through the health-insurance marketplace.
- Government programs such as Medicare, Medicaid, or the Children's Health Insurance Program (CHIP).
- The Veterans Administration or TRICARE for military personnel (might not be practical for you if you just coming into the country).
- Your state, if it provides an insurance plan.

- Continuing employer coverage from your former employer, on a temporary basis under the consolidated omnibus budget reconciliation act, also known as COBRA (might not be practical for you if you just settled into the country).

It is worth noting here that I obtained my first health-insurance coverage through my university, Bradley University. The school offered avenues for international students like me to be covered. The only issue here was it was expensive for me, because the premium had to be paid in full for the year, as opposed to monthly installment payments.

Be a partner with your health-care professionals

One of the things that remains a constant for me as a professional engineer is the constant challenges I face regardless of my experience in my field. Even similar projects that one could easily categorize as duplicates of prior ones are unique and pose their own unique set of problems.

I work with other professionals who sometimes look to me to provide certain answers, and oftentimes I am as clueless as they are, if not more clueless.

Doctors and health-care professionals are not excluded from the challenges of their everyday work. What separates professionals is the ability to find the answers and implement known solutions, or at least tested ones.

Doctors and health-care professionals don't know all the answers, and sometimes they are also clueless. Your ability and willingness to engage them, ask questions, listen to their responses, understand them, ask more questions, and develop a comprehensive understanding of what it is they are talking about are necessary for you to receive the best health-care plan and to know what you are getting out of any treatment.

Imagine going into surgery and instead of the surgeon removing only the appendix, he took the wrong initiative to remove the gall bladder. Let's just clarify that this is a BIG NO-NO!

My advice for you all is to know your doctor's plans and his or her understanding of any tests or assessments conducted.

Know the risks of the procedures to be carried out, their side effects, and any possible complications that could arise. To say it in one statement: *be fully aligned with your health-care professional!*

Food—the world is yours—really

Here is a table of ideas for available food in the United States. We are blessed here with all types of cuisines from all over the world, different food groups, exotic spices, fresh foods, hot meals, cold cuts—the list goes on and on. When it comes to food in America, the whole world is here, and the world is yours.

Thai	African	Soul Food
Seafood	Pizza	Southern
Fast food	American	Healthy
Burgers	Street food	Mexican
Italian	Salads	Chinese
Indian	Japanese	Vegan
Mediterranean	Sushi	Greek
Latin American	Gluten free	Cuban
French	Korean	Kosher
Vietnamese	Caribbean	Lebanese

Food—Delivered to your door

Again, the world is yours. There is so much food here in the States, so much variety, so many different ways to get the food to you. Below are some delivery services. You can download their apps to your mobile phone and take full advantage:

- Uber Eats
- Door Dash
- Grubhub
- Postmates
- CleanBite
- FoodMe
- Delivery.com
- Talabat
- Yummit
- SpoonRocket

This is just to name a few; however, I personally use Door Dash and Uber Eats. They seem to be the most available for me when I travel. I must say that I sometimes find Uber Eats' delivery fee quite expensive. The convenience of having any food you desire from your local area restaurants delivered to you in your home does have its appeal and comes in very handy. I use these services mostly during the winter months when going out in the cold weather...well, let's just say going hungry seems to be a better choice than stepping out. These food delivery companies have enhanced my life many times over.

A snapshot—my attempt at a healthy lifestyle

There are quite a number of ways to live a healthy lifestyle; however, I want to share with you what I have done over the years. You will see for yourself how it is an ever-evolving journey. For the years I have been in the United States:

- **Year one through year six**
  o I went to go to the gym about three or four times a week, for at least one hour. Oftentimes I spent two hours there with friends.
  o I engaged in weights, basketball, and swimming.
- **Year seven through year fifteen**
  o I went to the gym about three times a week, sometimes even less. At this point, it was a struggle balancing work and creating time for exercise.
- **Year sixteen**
  o I focused more on calisthenics and being conscious of what food I ate.
  o I started training for my first marathon races and half marathons.
- **Year seventeen**
  o I did running, stair climbing, and other aerobic activities.
- **Currently**
  o I do intermittent fasting (so many benefits here) coupled with aerobic exercises, and I'm conscious

about the food I put in my body—and, most importantly, vitamins.

This is just an account of what I have done over the years. More prevalent now is intermittent fasting, which gives my body a break from working breaking down food.

Exercise I enjoy

To share with you some of what I have done in the past and enjoyed:

Activity	My Take
Gym	Indoors, at a club like LA Fitness, I enjoy working on the upper body, doing pull-ups and other forms of calisthenics. Occasionally, I play racquetball with friends and colleagues.
Yoga	I used to belong to Core Power Yoga club. It is beneficial for me to stretch; anyone who knows me will testify to how flexible I am not. Also, yoga helps in my breathing, blood pressure, and focus. I personally enjoy their hot power fusion class.
Running	I have done two half marathons (13.1 miles/21.1 km) in Chicago and completed two full marathons (26.2 miles/42.2 km), one in Chicago and the other in Lisbon, Portugal. The entire training program promotes physical fitness and enhances you to be at your best on so many levels. The most important for me was discipline.
Stair Climbing	My favorite. This is a great exercise that allows you to do more work in half the time as running, and it builds lower body strength, your core, and your endurance. With stair climbing, you are fighting against gravity and vertical movement. I love Swallow Cliff in Palos Heights, Illinois, and Westcliff, Johannesburg.

I suggest you find out what it is you enjoy and do it. The only way would be for you to try as many activities as possible, both indoors and outdoors. Have fun doing it, make some friends, and most importantly, stay on top of your healthy active lifestyle.

Train for your first 5K (3.1 miles)

Making a 5K (3.1 miles) run as part of your lifestyle will yield significant health benefits, make you stronger, and keep you strong. From marathonrookie.com, this is a quick, easy enough starting guide for anyone without discrimination based on fitness level or physical attributes. It is the same plan I used to get myself off the couch and to the trail for my very first races.

	Week #1	Week #2	Week #3	Week #4	Week #5
Monday	Run/walk 15 mins	Run/walk 20 mins	Run/walk 25 mins	Run/walk 25 mins	Run/walk 20 mins
Tuesday	Run/walk 2 miles	Run/walk 2 miles	Run/walk 2 miles	Run/walk 2 miles	Run/walk 20 mins
Wednesday	rest day	rest day	rest day	rest day	rest day
Thursday	Run/walk 15 mins	Run/walk 20 mins	Run/walk 25 mins	Run/walk 30 mins	Run/walk 15 mins
Friday	rest day	rest day	rest day	rest day	rest day

Saturday	Run/walk 25 mins	Run/walk 35 mins	Run/ walk 30 mins	Run/ walk 45 mins	Run/walk 3.1 miles
Sunday	rest day	rest day	rest day	rest day	rest day

Study the plan, get moving, find the pace that gives you pleasure and not pain, and keep going. Keep going, be consistent, and believe in yourself. You will reap what you sow!

CHAPTER 4

Education in the USA

Introduction—quick facts

- Education in the United States is compulsory all the way up to the age of sixteen or eighteen years. This depends on the state you are a resident in.
- The academic year is mid-August/mid-September to mid-May/mid-June.
- The language of instruction is English.
- The total number of foreign students (international students) in the United States, counting all countries, as of the year 2016/2017, is about 1,078,822.

2016/2017 - Foreign students, 1,078,822

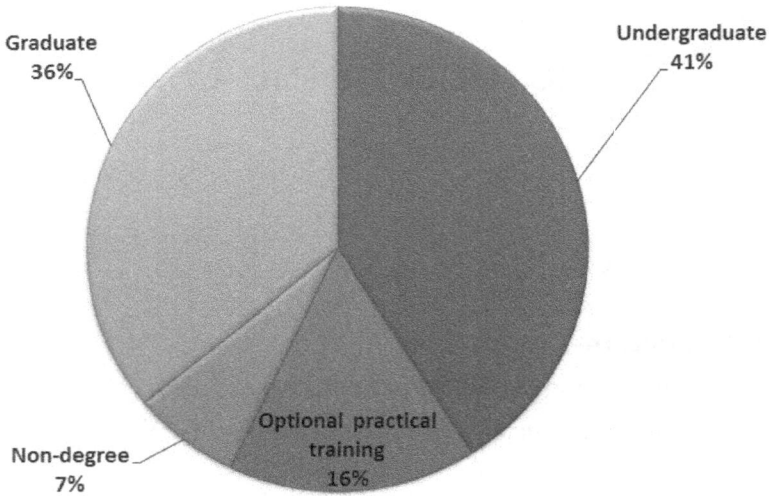

Graduate
36%

Undergraduate
41%

Non-degree
7%

Optional practical
training
16%

The education system in the United States

Below is a flowchart showing the different paths one can take in the education system in the United States. As you can see, they all end in one or two final goals, be it the university research doctoral degree or the university first professional degree. Either way, it is up to you how far you want to study or the path you'll take once you have achieved the minimum of a high school diploma.

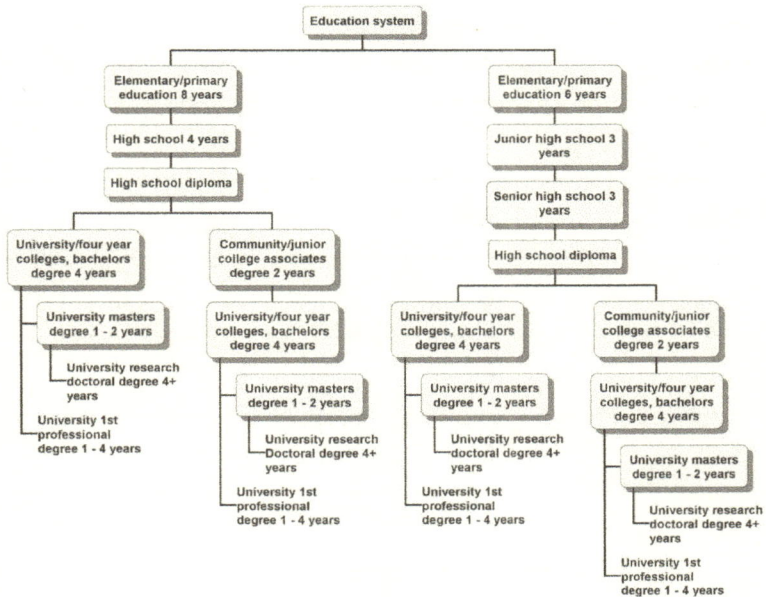

BEFORE YOU GO TO AMERICA

The grading scale in the United States

I wish I had been properly informed on the grading system in America. This would have saved me confusion and headaches. Below is a table of the grading scale most commonly used in colleges, with the percent grade and its corresponding grade on the 4.0 scale.

Percent grade	Letter grade	4.0 Scale (GPA)
93–100	A	4.0
90–92	A-	3.7
87–89	B+	3.3
83–86	B	3.0
80–82	B-	2.7
77–79	C+	2.3
73–76	C+	2.0
70–72	C-	1.7
67–69	D+	1.3
63–66	D+	1.0

60–62	D-	0.7
Below 60	F	0.0

It is worth mentioning that the three types of honors you can graduate with, depending on your grade point average (GPA), are cum laude (with honors/with praise), magna cum laude (with great honors/with great praise), and lastly, summa cum laude (with greatest honors/with greatest praise). The specific criteria are established by each school for choosing and awarding honors. Generally, minimum requirements are 3.4+ GPA for cum laude, 3.6+ GPA for magna cum laude, and 3.8+ for summa cum laude.

STEM education

I had the privilege of studying engineering, and I want to make sure I include some interesting facts about science, technology, engineering, and mathematics, also known as STEM. From my own personal observation from working in the manufacturing sector for several years, these are quite accurate.

7 Interesting facts about STEM Education	
At present, the number of unfilled STEM vacancies in the US is higher than the number of qualified candidates.	Salary: The average payout of STEM jobs is 70 percent more than the US national average.
Requirement: Kansas and Missouri will need 185,000 additional people with STEM education.	Growth: The department of commerce predicts that between 2008 and 2018, STEM jobs will grow twice as fast as other jobs.
Wanted: Eight out of the ten most-wanted employees listed by the US Department of Labor were those with a STEM education.	Future: The US Bureau of Statistics says that in the next twenty years, 80 percent of jobs will require technical skills.

Reality: STEM employees are in charge of building communities and moving the nation forward.	Lastly, from my own personal observation from working in the manufacturing sector for several years, these are quite accurate.

CHAPTER 5

The American Credit System

As a young boy just arriving in the United States, I quickly realized that I needed a means of transportation to go to certain places—for example, to buy groceries, to go to the post office... you get this gist. After going to the student center, I picked up a newspaper that had information about an auto dealership. I called them, made an appointment, and showed up. The car salesman was every bit of the cliché you would expect: he was nice, but he was determined that I make a deal and walk out of there with a car. Cutting this long story short, after a test drive, after choosing the car of my dreams, I decided it was time to make a choice. I chose. I was happy; I was excited.

We went inside the main office to sit down and draw up the paperwork and the application. He asked me for my Social Security number; I gave it to him without hesitation. After about ten minutes of waiting, he walked back in the office and told me he couldn't find me in the system, that I did not exist. Obviously

I was surprised. I said, "Am I not standing here physically?" This made no sense to me.

He then asked this series of questions: "Do you have a credit card? Do you have a house you pay a mortgage on? Have you ever borrowed money at an interest rate?" I said no to all these questions. He was like, "Well, you do not exist. You do not have any credit history, so we cannot trust you to give you an auto loan and close this deal." I was dismayed! I was devastated! After taking months of driving school and learning the rules of the road, after hours of searching for a car and taking a test drive and having daydreams of owning my first car, I met my first disappointment due to my lack of credit. This was my introduction to the importance of the American credit system. My choices at this point were to either pay the entire car payment in cash or have a cosigner who could use their good credit history to secure an auto loan for me.

What is credit? Why should you care?

The word *credit* in the United States is the term used to describe money you have borrowed from a credit grantor—for example, a bank—to purchase goods and services. I imagine that this definition holds true in most part of the world.

For example, you borrow $150,000 from a particular bank to buy your first home for your family. You will typically sign some form of binding legal agreement—a contract—to pay the grantor back at a specified interest rate over a predetermined length of time.

Now, as for the why, credit allows you to leverage money that is not your own—for example, the bank's money—to purchase goods and services you cannot afford to put all the money (100 percent) down on all at once.

Credit allows you to establish a history, which other lenders can use to establish your creditworthiness. By treating credit with respect and treating it properly, you can significantly increase your purchasing power exponentially.

In the United States of America, your credit is your identity. Never forget this.

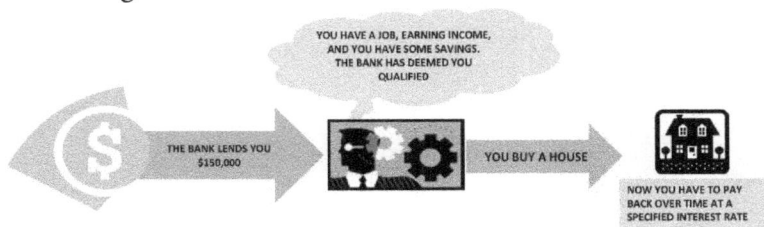

YOU HAVE A JOB, EARNING INCOME, AND YOU HAVE SOME SAVINGS. THE BANK HAS DEEMED YOU QUALIFIED

THE BANK LENDS YOU $150,000

YOU BUY A HOUSE

NOW YOU HAVE TO PAY BACK OVER TIME AT A SPECIFIED INTEREST RATE

The types of credit

There are four main types of credit, and they are the following:

1. **Revolving credit**: An example is most credit cards. You are given a maximum credit limit, and then you spend using the credit line and card. You then must make a payment every month. This type of credit is to be used with care, its usage must be kept to a minimum, and you must make payments on time.

2. **Charge cards**: This is very similar to revolving credit; however, every month you must make the payment of the entire balance on the credit line and card. Again, avoid excess, minimize usage, and do not exceed 10 percent of your approved limit.

3. **Service credit**: Examples are utility bills, electricity, cell phone service, gym memberships, and general agreements with service providers. Make payments on time.

4. **Installment credit**: These are car loans and mortgages on houses. A creditor lends you an amount that you agree to pay in regular installments of a fixed amount over a fixed length of time, with interest.

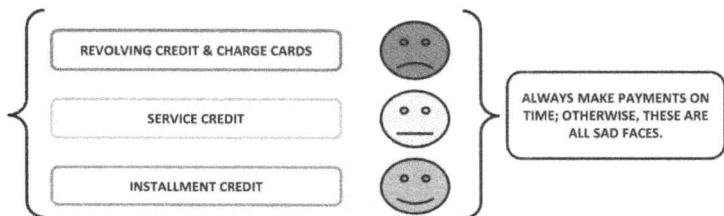

REVOLVING CREDIT & CHARGE CARDS

SERVICE CREDIT

INSTALLMENT CREDIT

ALWAYS MAKE PAYMENTS ON TIME; OTHERWISE, THESE ARE ALL SAD FACES.

What is a credit score?

Your credit score is a three-digit number that represents how likely you are to pay your bills. Credit grantors, banks, and the like, use this three-digit number to decide whether they will approve you for a new credit card or any other type of loan. The score is based on credit-report information from one of the three major credit bureaus:

1. Experian
2. Transunion
3. Equifax

Below is a table providing you with more details on the credit bureaus, their scoring ranges, and the scales they use to determine poor, fair, good, and excellent credit scores. Ultimately, this is used to inform the credit grantors of your creditworthiness.

Credit Bureau	Range	Poor	Fair	Good	Excellent
Experian	300–850	300–579	580–669	670–799	800–850
Transunion	300–850	300–600	601–660	661–780	781–850
Equifax	300–850	300–600	601–660	661–780	781–850

What factors affect your credit score?

You should know that there are six main factors that have an impact on your credit score. You must understand these factors so that you are able to manage them effectively and maintain a very healthy and strong credit score and report. The table below breaks these down so you can easily digest them. However, it is worth defining for you what a hard pull and a soft pull into your credit history are. These are both inquiries into your credit history by any interested party. A soft pull does not affect your credit score. It shows summary information on your credit background, and it is mostly done as a background check. A hard pull is done into your credit history by lenders who are trying to approve a loan or a line of credit, to inform them of your creditworthiness, and this will affect your credit history and score.

Factors	Impact to your credit	My personal recommendations for you
Hard inquiries into your credit report from grantors and other interested parties	LOW	Manage this to three hard pulls or fewer per 2 years. So do not have ten credit-card applications out there. Retail stores like to ask you to open a new card to get a store discount. Refrain from this.
The total number of credit accounts that you have	LOW	Use a variety of accounts responsibly. You can have about five to twelve credit accounts of different credit types

The age of your entire credit history (average of age of all accounts). Basically, how long you have had credit	MEDIUM	Start to establish your credit as early as possible, even if it's just a small account. You want the overall average age of your credit to be at least five years old, if not more.
Derogatory marks on your credit history and report	HIGH	Try to avoid any derogatory remarks on your report. Manage to one, best that there are none.
Credit-card utilization	HIGH	Manage this to achieve 10 percent utilization or less of the total balance of all approved credit limits.
Your overall payment history. Basically, on-time and late payments	HIGH	Pay your bills on time to achieve greater than 98 percent on-time payments of your report.

How to establish credit now and maintain it

What no one will tell you, but I am taking the time to reveal, is that even if you don't need credit yet, start establishing credit as soon as possible. Remember, the age of your credit history is a contributing factor to the strength and health of your credit report and score. The table below tells you step by step what to do to get your credit in good shape. Start establishing credit now so you can begin leveraging your borrowing power to facilitate your wealth growth.

Step 1: Establish your credit	Step 2: Build Your score with good habits	Step 3: Monitor your scores and reports
1. Apply for a secured credit card or loan. For example, open a secured card with openskycc.com. It is backed by a cash deposit you make up front, and it's easy to qualify.	1. Make 100 percent of your payments on time, including utility bills.	1. Sign up at the Credit Karma website and download the mobile application. It is free of charge, it does a soft pull on your credit, and it provides you with two scores out of three from the credit bureaus.

2. Apply for a credit builder loan. It will help build your credit	2. Keep credit utilization low. Best practice is anywhere from 10 percent to 20 percent. Utilization is how much of your approved credit limit you are using. So if you have a $100 credit card, 10 percent utilization is keeping purchases no more than $10.	2. Sign up at the Experian website. This is also free and gives you a score and report from Experian.
3. Become an authorized user on someone else's credit card. Make sure the card issuer reports authorized user activity to the credit bureaus.	3. Avoid opening too many new accounts at once. New accounts lower your average account age.	3. Sign up with Nerd Wallet. This is also free. This will educate you on the different financial services and products in the market.
4. Get a cosigner for a small loan or an unsecured credit card.	4. Keep accounts for as long as possible, for the sake of your length of payment history and utilization.	4. Sign up with Procredit.com. This is a paid service; however, it does a soft pull and provides all three scores from the credit bureau.
5. Get credit for the rent you are already paying. Use a rent-reporting service like Rental Kharma and Rent Track to help build a positive history of on-time payments.	5. Check each of your credit reports annually for errors and discrepancies so you can dispute them and remove them from your report. Beware and protect yourself from identity theft.	5. You are allowed one free report every year from each of the three credit bureaus, so you should request them. Order online from annualcreditreport.com, or call 1-877-322-8228.

CHAPTER 6

Money and Wealth

What is financial intelligence?

Intelligence is the acquisition of data and information for the sole purpose of enabling whoever is collecting it to initiate and execute powerful actions that lead to a desired outcome. Applying this definition, we can define financial intelligence as the foundational understandings of the inner workings of the financial world that enable you to grow your wealth and expand your portfolio. You can have an accounting or finance degree but still lack financial intelligence. If you do not use the data gathered and information collected to achieve powerful personal results for you, you lack financial intelligence.

This is not a fancy definition or a complex one. Financial intelligence for you and your family is the understanding of financial and accounting principles and understanding how money is being used so you can leverage it to grow your wealth.

Basic Definitions:

Now on to basic definitions as I understand them (not textbook definitions):

- **Income**: This is earnings that have monetary value from goods or services sold. It is a positive inflow of money to your account. Example: salary and wages from your job.
- **Expense**: Whatever you spend your money on that does not add value to your financial portfolio is an expense. It does not increase the worth of anything in your portfolio.
- **Asset**: This is anything of value that puts money into your pocket. It is usually tangible, either physically, such as a rental property, or it exists in digital space, such as stock in a company.
- **Asset allocation**: This is the percentage of each asset type you have in your portfolio, such as stocks, bonds, and real estate. Usually the percentage target—your target allocation—is based on how much risk you would like to tolerate for your entire portfolio.
- **Liabilities**: Keeping this simple, this takes money out of your pocket and must be serviced. It usually doesn't add value, but it must be paid—for example, an electric bill for a home you have or a debt payment for a car loan.
- **Accounting**: To keep it simple, this is the methods, systems, and processes that capture your entire financial landscape and cash flow, both in and out.

- **Investing**: This is the process of staking your money down with the hope that it increases in value due to this money working for you. For example, you buy shares of a company for ten dollars per share, and in five years' time, the same company is selling its shares for twenty dollars. You have doubled your money, doubled your investments. Investments can be collateralized or not.
- **Cash flow**: This is the flow of money either into your pocket or out of your pocket over a given period of time. This is the kinetic energy of money. It is usually affected by income, assets, debts, liabilities, and expenses.
- **Levers of wealth**: These are income, savings, and expenses. To achieve real wealth, all three levers must be operated and be under your command and control. Increase your income, increase your savings, and minimize your expenses.
- **Stocks**: This is a type of investment that allows you to own portions of a company. You are buying a small piece of the company, called a share.
- **Bonds**: This is a type of investment in which you are giving the issuer of the bond a loan, and they agree to pay it back at a fixed rate on a specific date.
- **Dividends**: Dividends are rewards paid by a company to the owners of stocks, also known as shareholders, based on that company's earnings. For example, Apple Inc. pays two dollars per share owned.

- **Compounding:** Imagine earning interest on your principal, and then this interest earns interest, as it is now added to the principal and reinvested. This is the power of compounding, and it exponentially accelerates growth.

- **Cost of living:** This is how much it costs you to live in a particular area or city. Things such as housing, transportation, and shopping vary from city to city, and the overall cost is known as the cost of living.

- **Mortgage:** A mortgage is a loan taken out by you, approved by a lender, for the sole purpose of buying real estate. This usually is given to you at a fixed rate over a specified time, and monthly installments to include principal and interest are paid back to the lender for the duration of the mortgage.

Basic rules I follow for a financial intelligence foundation

These simple laws were obtained from several books that I have read—to name a couple, *Rich Dad Poor Dad*, by Robert Kiyosaki, and *Financial Freedom*, by Grant Sabatier.

- **Save Early**: This goes without saying. Investment really isn't about the time when you buy or sell an asset. It's really about how long you have been in the market. Saving early buys you as much time as you can get to start to let your money work for you.
- **Live considerably below your means**: Really, do I have to say this? LOL. Okay, please live below your means, and not beyond them. Spend a considerably less amount than what you are bringing in, so as to have more money for investments. Once you are able to achieve this, you will have more cash in hand, and you will be able to invest it.
- **Pay yourself first:**[1] As you earn income from whatever source, you must pay yourself first before any other person, entity, or government. This ensures you always get paid. Learn to withstand the financial pressure of others needing to be paid. This pressure unlocks your

---

1 Robert T. Kiyosaki and Sharon L. Lechter, *Rich Dad, Poor Dad: What the Rich Teach Their Kids about Money—That the Poor and Middle Class Do Not!* (Warner, 2000), 78–80.

creative genius to find out how to make more money and pay them.

- **Understand your cash flow:** How can you be wealthy and not know your numbers—your cash flow? You must know the fixed numbers of how much money you make, be it from income or investments, and how much money you spend, be it expenses or liabilities. You cannot control what you do not measure.

- **Minimize your expenses:** Keep expenses as low as possible. Go out and enjoy that Starbucks coffee when you want, but overall, be mindful. This is critical to operating one of the levers of wealth to your advantage.

- **Eliminate your debts:** Read this as it is written. Eliminate your debts, especially the very bad ones that do nothing for your financial portfolio, such as credit cards. These are useless debts, and they have damaging consequences.

- **Pay down the least amount of debt first:** Debt elimination is not an easy task, so go after the low-hanging fruit first. This will also give you that sense of accomplishment, and you can get right back to working on debt elimination.

- **Mind your business:**[2] Okay, I want to keep this simple enough. Whatever it is that brings you money outside of your regular job is your business, and you should mind

---

2 Kiyosaki and Lechter, *Rich Dad*, 43–47.

it. Your regular job is a job, and it's not your business unless you own the company, which I doubt! So, mind the things that you own, that generate income for you and your family. Mind your business with the goal of sustainability, expansion, and growing your business.

Investment portfolio theories

There are two portfolio theories I want to introduce to you, and that's the traditional and the modern theories. The only difference, basically, is that the traditional portfolio theory solely advocates for stocks and bonds, whereas the modern advocates for including some real estate in your portfolio, at about a 30 percent asset allocation.

Let's illustrate these concepts with pie charts:

Traditional portfolio theory

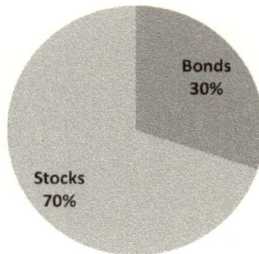

Modern portfolio theory

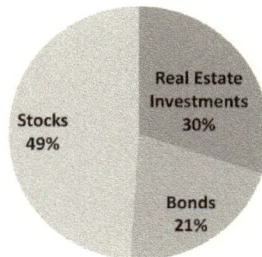

Open and structure your bank accounts this way

Most banks will allow you to open multiple checking accounts, and all will be easily accessible to you via their online banking or mobile banking applications. This will help you segregate your money into what I call buckets. This way you can move money into the other accounts from your master, insulating your master account. I use PNC Bank and Chase.

Action: Open five checking accounts at the same bank and then nickname them as below.

CHECKING ACCOUNT - MASTER ACCOUNT (ALL MONEY COMES IN HERE)
This is the first account where all your money will be deposited. Only you should have access to this account to move money out to the other accounts. This will help with paying yourself first.

CHECKING ACCOUNT - DEBT SERVICE
This account is for things like home mortgage payments, student loans, car loans, and other debts that need to be serviced.

CHECKING ACCOUNT - BILLS & EXPENSES
This is for things like insurance payments, utility bills, monthly subscription services, etc.

CHECKING ACCOUNT - DISCRETIONARY SPEND
This is your money for other things, like a petty cash account. It will be used for your monthly spending like restaurants, coffee, etc. (Estimate and fund it).

CHECKING ACCOUNT - UNFORESEEN SPEND
Any unforeseen spending, that you need but is not reoccurring—car repair, kitchen upgrade. Usually these spends are large, but this account will help you save and plan for them.

Why, you might ask, should you open this many accounts and then structure them this way? The truth is, you do not need to. I am only sharing with you what has worked for me and the benefits I have been able to enjoy.

Structuring your accounts this way allows you to fully control your cash flow and make allocations to the different buckets of accounts based on what is needed at fixed intervals. It also insulates your master account by ensuring only you have access to the account where your money flows in. For example, an auto-pay transaction for a car loan will only be able to access the debt service account, which you move money into yourself when you decide to. This also insulates you from potentially fraudulent activities.

How I use my checking accounts (what I do)

Below is a self-explanatory diagram that attempts to show the flow of money into and out of the master account. As you can see from the image below, all interface of money coming out of the master account is via one of the other accounts that must be funded by me. This way, my master account, where my money flows in, is insulated from cash moving out to the outside world.

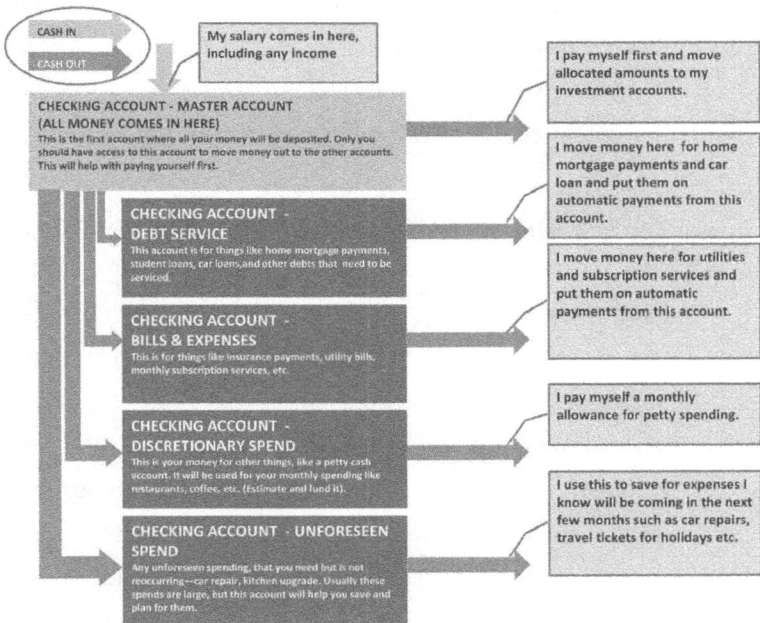

CASH IN

CASH OUT

My salary comes in here, including any income

CHECKING ACCOUNT - MASTER ACCOUNT
(ALL MONEY COMES IN HERE)
This is the first account where all your money will be deposited. Only you should have access to this account to move money out to the other accounts. This will help with paying yourself first.

CHECKING ACCOUNT - DEBT SERVICE
This account is for things like home mortgage payments, student loans, car loans, and other debts that need to be serviced.

CHECKING ACCOUNT - BILLS & EXPENSES
This is for things like insurance payments, utility bills, monthly subscription services, etc.

CHECKING ACCOUNT - DISCRETIONARY SPEND
This is your money for other things, like a petty cash account. It will be used for your monthly spending like restaurants, coffee, etc. (Estimate and fund it).

CHECKING ACCOUNT - UNFORESEEN SPEND
Any unforeseen spending, that you need but is not reoccurring—car repair, kitchen upgrade. Usually these spends are large, but this account will help you save and plan for them.

I pay myself first and move allocated amounts to my investment accounts.

I move money here for home mortgage payments and car loan and put them on automatic payments from this account.

I move money here for utilities and subscription services and put them on automatic payments from this account.

I pay myself a monthly allowance for petty spending.

I use this to save for expenses I know will be coming in the next few months such as car repairs, travel tickets for holidays etc.

Open these accounts for investments (what I have)

1. **Betterment**: This is a robo-adviser for investments. It allows you to set your portfolio and risk threshold based on percentages and allocations, and you will be leveraged in both small and large markets. You are able to trade stocks, bonds, and ETFs. There is a small fee of about 0.25 percent of the balance annually (as of 2019), but it's a small price to pay to get you started in investments.
   a. **Alternative**: Wealthfront
   b. **Website**: www.betterment.com, www.wealthfront.com

2. **Robinhood**: This is an online brokerage platform that has no transaction fees; however, it doesn't have extensive research capabilities, and it's just pure trading of stocks, bonds, ETFs, and now cryptocurrencies such as bitcoins and ethereum.
   a. **Website**: www.robinhood.com

3. **Acorns**: Set up an account here, and tie it to your most widely used checking account or accounts. This account rounds up every transaction you make to the nearest dollar and moves those small amounts to an investment account, and you won't even notice it working for you.
   a. **Website**: www.acorns.com

4. **TDAmeritrade/Charles Schwab**: For the most serious trading and investments, this is where you want to be. It is an online brokerage firm that puts a full range of research and analytical capabilities at your disposal. You are able to trade stocks, bonds, ETFs, and more. It has mobile applications, web applications, and even desktop applications for speed. It is worth mentioning that Charles Schwab has now acquired TDAmeritrade.

    a. **Alternative**: E*TRADE (subsidiary of Morgan Stanley)

    b. **Website**: www.TDAmeritrade.com, www.Schwab.com, www.Etrade.com

5. **Fundrise**: Keep this simple: this is for investing in private REITs (real estate investment trusts). This investment instrument used to be for the wealthy, but now anyone can start real estate investments with as little as $500. Your portfolio is diversified across several properties all over the country, and returns are in the form of dividends and asset appreciation.

    a. **Website**: www.fundrise.com

How I use my investment accounts (what I do)

Investment accounts	What to do with them
Betterment	When I pay myself first, I put 70 percent of the funds in this account. My portfolio here is set up as 90 percent stocks and 10 percent bonds.
Robinhood	Ten percent of what's left after other investment accounts are funded goes into this account.
Acorns	This is linked to my most-used checking account, and it's funded automatically by rounding up my transactions and moving the difference into the account.
TDAmeritrade	I use this primarily for the purchase of long-term stocks and for research of companies, funds, stocks, and bonds. I usually make large purchases that have been thoroughly investigated here for long-term acquisition, with the dividend reinvestment feature enabled.
Fundrise	When I pay myself first, I put 20 percent of the funds into this account. My portfolio here is set up as a balanced one. This has a 3–7 investment horizon as opposed to daily liquidity.

Important notes

I use the modern portfolio theory for the most part. I have allocated 20 percent (adjusted from 30 percent) into private real estate investments, and the remaining 80 percent is in stocks and bonds across different brokerages. This allows me flexibility while diversifying. Also, as of the time I am writing this, I am monitoring the performances of the different platforms. As with anything that you want to make better, this will need to be tweaked as time progresses.

What I aim to offer you here is a starting point, without you thinking about what to do. These are entry-level approaches to investments and will carry you for many years as you continue to expand on your own knowledge and experiences.

There are many investment vehicles, and it is ultimately up to you to have a plan and a vision and continue to evaluate them periodically and adjust them to meet your goals and desired outcome.

Key Concepts: Retirement accounts

Everyone must prepare for retirement. It is only good practice. The American system has several options you can leverage for yourself and your family, and I will describe only a few below.

- **401(k) accounts**: These are retirement accounts usually offered through one job and employer. It allows for you to make contributions into the account via pretax income (this helps to reduce overall adjusted gross income) up to a certain maximum allowed by the government. This maximum as of 2020 is about $19,500 annually for an individual contribution, and $26,000 if you are age fifty or older. Usually, employers that offer this also offer a match to your contribution, and this varies across employers. I personally have had employers match my contribution dollar for dollar up to 6 percent of my salary. Deductions and withdrawals will be taxed, and early withdrawal before retirement might carry penalties.

- **Traditional IRAs (individual retirement accounts)**: Usually this is offered outside of employers, by financial institutions, for retirement purposes. It also provides tax advantages, as contributions to this account are from pretax income. This offers tax deferments, as withdrawals are taxed at a later date. The maximum allowed by the government as of 2020 is $6,000 annually per individual, or $7,000 if you are age fifty or older. This type of account is limited to certain individuals depending on income.

- **Roth IRAs**: This is similar to the traditional IRAs and differs only in the fact that contributions to this account are made with after-tax dollars. This type of account has the advantage of offering tax-free growth, thereby acting as a tax shelter.

What to do:

1. Make sure you max out all contributions to all retirement accounts based on employer matching contributions and allowable maximums annually.
2. Depending on your salary, if you are taxed at 25 percent and up, prioritize the 401(k) and the traditional IRA.
3. If your tax bracket is less than 25 percent, prioritize the Roth IRA.
4. Continue to monitor these accounts and understand their asset allocations and adjust as necessary to fit your needs.
5. Consult with experienced brokers and financial advisers for more information.

Key Concepts: The levers of wealth

According to Grant Sabatier, author of the book *Financial Freedom*, there are three basic variables to wealth, and he calls them levers:

1. **Income**: how much money you earn
2. **Savings**: how much money you set aside that can be invested
3. **Expenses**: how much money you are spending[3]

So, your goals are as follows:

1. Increase and maximize your income.
2. Increase and maximize your savings.
3. Reduce and, if possible, eliminate your expenses.

All three levers, when working for you, are the key to your financial freedom. Know this concept, and over time, as your knowledge continues to grow, your applications will effortlessly yield great returns for you and your family.

---

3 Grant Sabatier and Vicki Robin, *Financial Freedom: A Proven Path to All the Money You Will Ever Need* (Avery, 2019), 93.

Key concept: cash flow quadrants

Robert Kiyosaki, the author of *Rich Dad Poor Dad*, highlighted the concept of cash flow quadrants. This concept identifies the sources of wealth and income for any one individual.

1. **E Quadrant—Employee:** This is the quadrant where one has a standard 9–5, M–F job and earns a salary. This is the most taxed.

2. **S Quadrant—Self-Employed:** These are the people who have small and self-managed businesses and earn revenue. However, these businesses are totally dependent on the owner being fully present and require their employment 100 percent of the time.

3. **B Quadrant—Business Owner:** These are the people who own businesses. Their job is to dream up a business, execute it, leave it to capable managers and operators, and then move on to the next business venture. Their businesses do not depend on them being present day in, day out.

4. **I Quadrant—Investor:** These people make money exclusively from their investments, be it dividends from stocks and bonds, real estate rental income, or royalties from intellectual properties owned by them.[4]

---

4   Robert T. Kiyosaki, *Rich Dad's CASHFLOW Quadrant* (Plata Publishing, 2011), 1.

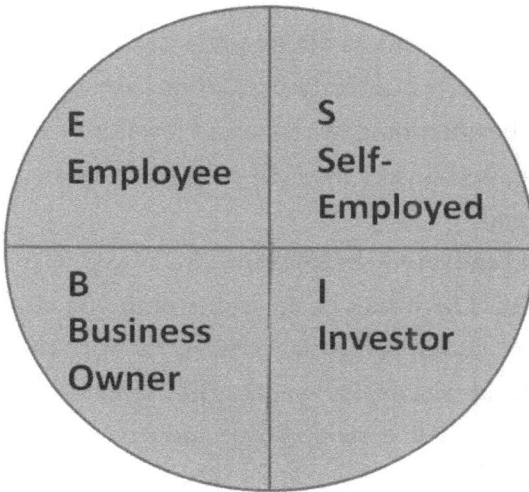

You all must know these quadrants, and in our world today, you must exist in all four quadrants, with a bias toward existing in the B and I quadrants. This should be your mission.

How to exist in any of the cash-flow quadrants

Okay, so we have talked about some key concepts. You now know what the four cash flow quadrants are and their definitions, but the question now remains: How does one exist in any of these quadrants? Let me help with some ideas to stimulate your thoughts.

1. **E Quadrant—Employee:** This is easy. *Get a job!* LOL. Okay, that being said, you should go to job fairs, search company websites, network through family and friends, and get that job. This is the job that will make you an employee and pay you a monthly wage or salary. Education is important, and the level to which one is educated matters in regard to what job you are able to get. A strong foundation and background are necessary, and a powerful network will help you here.

2. **S Quadrant—Self-Employed:** Depending on your education, your experience, and the skills you possess, you can start a small business where these same skill sets are on loan to other companies or outfits. For example, a medical doctor can exist both in the E quadrant as an employee at a hospital and also in the S quadrant as a consulting physician at other hospitals. He or she is not yet in the B quadrant because this company requires his direct skill set.

3. **B Quadrant—Business Owner:** Start a business of any sort. Start trading, buying, and selling commodities or services. Hire capable people to run your business, and free yourself to think up new ideas and start new businesses. If you have the capital, you can acquire an existing business with solid financials with the goal of expansion. In this quadrant, your job is to start the business and then move on.

4. **I Quadrant—Investor:** This is where the wealthy reside. Their income is mostly from investments. You can start by trading in stocks, bonds, and money market accounts. You can purchase income-generating assets and real estate for rental purposes. Stocks and bonds will pay you dividends and appreciate in value. With real estate you can get rental income, and it also appreciates in value.

You can invest in other income-generating assets such as businesses that do not require your presence, mutual funds, and royalties from intellectual property such as books, music, patents, and more. As Robert Kiyosaki says, "And anything else that has value, produces income or appreciates and has a ready market."[5]

---

5 Kiyosaki and Lechter, *Rich Dad*, 45.

Side hustle

It wouldn't be fair if I didn't talk briefly about this. As most of you have now realized, we are in a multiple-stream-of-income environment and also the sharing economy.

Side hustling is anything else you do outside of your main job that brings money into your pocket. The main goal of side hustling is to generate as much cash as you can, with the goal of investing this cash. Examples of what you could do for side hustling include but are not limited to the following:

- Website creation for small businesses
- Dog walking
- Babysitting
- Lawn mowing
- Ride-share driving (Uber, Lyft)
- Airbnb cohosting
- Airbnb arbitrage (renting a place and then hosting it while paying rent; the excess is profit)
- Deliveries of items; courier service
- Private application development
- Coding for small businesses
- Writing
- Photography
- Marketing
- Tutoring English, math, or any topic you are qualified for

- Consulting for other companies using your skills in your daytime job
- Trading items on Amazon, eBay, and so on
- Focus group participation
- Doing research
- Launching online classes

Once you decide you want or need a side hustle, you must evaluate its moneymaking potential, and then you determine what price you would like to charge.

Start an emergency fund

An emergency fund is exactly what is it called—a fund for emergency situations. What makes this fund unique is that it's usually very liquid and easily accessible, and it should not take more than three days to get the cash in your hands when you need it. Depending on your situation, this fund is usually four to six times your monthly expenditures. It is usually tapped into in the event of the loss of one's primary source of income. This fund is your survival kit, and it can be accumulated gradually. Once you hit the target amount, stop and do not touch it. It is a fund to support your bare-bones survival and should be available to you for your use. Some families do this collectively in a common wealth account, others individually, and sometimes even both. I suggest at a minimum, individually.

So, this is how you do it:

1. Determine how much you spend on rent or mortgage.
2. Determine how much you spend on basic utilities—electricity, water, and so on. Do not include premium cable channels.
3. Determine how much you spend on shopping for food and groceries. Do not include restaurants.
4. Determine how much you need for transportation, be it your car payments with fuel or the cost of the bus or train.
5. Total all the numbers you have.

6. Multiply this number by six, for six months of survival. This final amount is your target amount. This is the amount you need to raise and lock up, but make it easily accessible.

This fund will come in handy, and it will give you peace of mind and buy you time to get back on your feet should the need arise.

It must be treated with care, urgency, and respect to accumulate. This is not a fund for lending money to family or friends, and for all practical purposes, it is unavailable to you until an emergency.

I personally funded my emergency fund by driving an Uber taxi around the city of Chicago and setting aside 5 percent of my monthly paycheck into this fund to accelerate the time it would take to reach my target. When I was done, I moved the funds into a savings account with my brokerage firm that is easily accessible by me. I have had the need for this fund on several occasions—at the loss of my job, when I changed jobs, and even when I lost my mother while I was traveling and needed to raise cash fast.

Key concept: know your cash flow

You now know what cash flow is. It is the movement of money in and out of your account during a particular period—for example, your monthly cash flow. It is important for you to know your cash flow, because you cannot control what you do not measure. How would you know how to operate the levers of wealth if you do not know how much you make monthly or where your money is going? How would you know how much money you can save?

Here are the basic steps you need to take to know your cash flow. This is the beginning of commanding the levers of your wealth.

1. **Determine cash flow in**
   a. How much are you making monthly from your job?
   b. How much money are you earning from your side hustles?
   c. How much money are you making from your investments?
   d. Add these up, and this is your cash flow in.
2. **Determine cash flow out (debts, bills, discretionary and unforeseen expenses)**
   a. Debt servicing such as mortgage payments and car payments.
   b. Rent for your housing needs.
   c. Utilities.

    d. Subscriptions you are enrolled in, such as Amazon, cable service, and so on.

    e. Add these up, and this is your cash flow out.

3. **Do the math:** CASH FLOW IN – CASH FLOW OUT = NET CASH FLOW

This number should be positive. If it is not, guess what? You are spending more money than you are making, and this should be fixed immediately.

Coupled with this book is my simple Excel tool for the monthly management of my cash flow (download at http://www.verticalos.com). You are welcome to use it, and it's quite simple. It will allow you to see exactly where your money is going and will also assist you with planning to optimize or influence your cash flow for the coming months.

Cash flow management can get really serious, especially for businesses small and large. There are multiple analyses that can be done, but guess what? You do not need that now if you cannot get the basic subtraction of the money you are making minus the money you are spending on lockdown.

Cash flow management with software: for small businesses

This book is really for your own person; however, in the event some readers are well advanced and have accelerated their finances to exist in the B quadrant or the S quadrant, I want to introduce you to software tools that can aid you in your small-business finance and cash flow management. This will supercharge your accounting and also help you with your taxes. And if you have any independent contractors, well, guess what? They help you too.

The two software packages I have exposure to are the following:

1. **Intuit QuickBooks—Simple start**
   a. $12.50 to $25/month
   b. https://quickbooks.intuit.com
2. **Hurdlr–Premium**
   a. $7.99/month
   b. https://www.hurdlr.com

Both have the following capabilities:

   c. auto-expense tracking
   d. auto-income tracking
   e. capturing and organizing receipts
   f. real-time calculations for state and self-employment taxes
   g. running reports

h. managing contractors

i. desktop, online, and mobile applications

Of the two, I use Hurdlr for most of my small-business finances because it is easier for me to use, and I understand their platform much better. Not to take anything from QuickBooks. QuickBooks is very powerful and has many options—I would say this is the pro option.

With Hurdlr or QuickBooks, I can tie the platform to any of my bank accounts. They automatically capture my transactions, and I am able to tag them as personal or business. You can also have more than one business, and these transactions can be split across personal use or many businesses.

For those of you interested in finding out more, I would advise you to check both of these out and see how you can take advantage of their powerful tools to supercharge your cash flow management. The management of personal finance should be fun and should unlock your genius wherever you see roadblocks. Discover how you can make more money, how you can save more, and how you can always spend less. Cheers!

Automation of cash flow: savings, debts, and expenses

I think it would be useful to briefly discuss automatic transactions from your accounts. I'm referring to two categories, savings and expenses, which, as you recall, are two of the three levers of wealth. I initially was against any automatic withdrawals from my account, because I wanted to ensure I knew exactly where my money was going and, most importantly, when it was going. This way I am able to make the most of the little cash I have and decide who gets paid when.

The issue with this approach, as you might have guessed, is the possibility of late or missed payments, which can put your financial strength at risk, sometimes with late fees or canceled services or subscriptions, and even sometimes affecting your creditworthiness. Hence, the multiple checking accounts are segregated into buckets dedicated to their purposes.

So here is what I have done/do:

1. I know my cash flow, both in and out. I know the different amounts for debt servicing, bills, and expenses, and how much I would like to spend personally. Debt servicing are loans that have been granted to me at a specific interest rate, and monthly payments are made to the lender throughout the life of the loan.

2. I have decided what I want to pay myself, and I do pay myself first. I have automatic transfers scheduled to move what I want to pay myself first from my

master checking account into my investments account, based on my rules and portfolio allocations.

3. I have set up, for my bills and expenses, automatic
   payments with the companies in question. However,
   these payments are tied to the checking account
   dedicated to bills and expenses. This account is also
   funded whenever I am ready. This caters to me still
   controlling my money and the time when it goes out,
   and it also satisfies the vendors with auto payments.

4. I also have set up, for debt servicing, automatic payments via the checking account dedicated to that
   purpose. This way, I reduce the risk significantly of
   missed payments, thereby reducing any risk to my
   credit worthiness. By now you know why credit is
   important. The table below is a quick view of some of
   the pros and cons of setting up automatic payments
   for paying bills.

Pros	Cons	Solution to Cons
It's convenient.	You do not get a final confirmation before money goes.	Your confirmation is knowing your cash flow and then funding from your master account to other sub accounts.
It reduces stress.	You can get lazy with your money.	Knowing your cash flow is everything.

It mitigates if not eliminates late fees.	It can cause an overdraft in your account if it's not funded on time.	Again, know your cash flow, and fund your subaccounts.

How do you start earning money now?

Many of you are probably wondering right about now, How do I get that first job? How do I get my first job with little or no experience? This is a big question, and it determines the next few years of your financial future.

Getting a job in the United States—really, anywhere—is about developing your personal brand. According to professional coach Linda Raynier (you should check out her YouTube channel), personal branding is the impression of who you are, what you are capable of, and what makes you valuable. Personal brand has nothing to do with experience; it is much more than your resume and interviews. It is about positioning and selling yourself, persuading a prospective employer to hire you despite your lack of experience.

The goal is raising as much cash as you can as quickly as you can, and using this cash to invest in income-generating assets for you and your family. So, you see, getting a job and earning steady pay is the fastest way to get cash and then leverage it to continue to build your assets column. The overall message in this chapter focuses on understanding your money and your cash flow and using it wisely to build up your asset base. However, what is the point of all that talk if you do not have any money to pay your bills with or purchase assets? The following pages attempt to help you understand the opportunities out there and make the most of them. You are new here in the United States and most likely didn't go to school here, and you have little or no experience in the industries here. Perhaps you are a spouse of a foreign expert worker here; you should also have the avenue of making your own money and contributing to the financial success of the family and even building your own financial independence. Whether you are hoping to get a professional job or start your own business, these next pages are for you. Enjoy!

Your job search toolbox—what you should have in it?
The tools you need, or at least should have, in your toolbox are as follows:

1. Create a killer resume with a killer cover letter.
    a. Introduce yourself with a short profile summary.
    b. You should position yourself with the keywords and key phrases of the job for which you are applying.
    c. Every job you are interested in must have its own customized resume and cover letter.
    d. All dates included in your resume must be easy to understand and accurate.
    e. State your accomplishments in all relevant roles you have held anywhere, and avoid soft skills or job duties. Imagine a resume with a candidate's job duties; however, this person never even showed up to work in his or her previous roles.
    f. Use bullets, not paragraphs.
    g. Proofread and make necessary edits in all documents every time before you send them out anywhere, in person or online.
2. Research companies thoroughly before any interviews, by phone or in person. You must know these companies inside and out—what they are about, their

mission statements, their corporate social responsibilities, their product and/or service portfolios, and also their financial health. This will make you stand out from the crowd, and it will create top-of-mind awareness among the directors and executives who will interview you.

3. Practice interview questions. Practice, practice, and practice some more. This will make you a pro. There will be a point when all this just comes very naturally to you.

4. Dress professionally for all interviews, no matter what they tell you. Some interviewers will request you dress business casual. My advice: always dress professionally, and you most certainly can't go wrong. Underdress and you risk not using the opportunity to create a lasting impression. I remember a young man I interviewed for a plant engineering role. All we required was a polo shirt and jeans; however, this gentleman showed up in a business suit and killer well-polished shoes. This was what everyone was talking about afterward—and his experience, of course.

5. Know the role you are applying for and what is expected of you. Always ask what will be expected of you that isn't being done at the moment and that only you or your position can do.

6. Lastly, remember that you are being interviewed and also interviewing the company and the team in which you will be working. It is vital that you belong. I once interviewed for a company (no names here) where they did a bait and switch on me as to who exactly I would be working for. It turned out that my superior and I didn't fit in the slightest. I quit this job after only four months. This could easily have been avoided if I had asked the right questions.

Steps to getting that first job with little or no experience

I want to recommend the following steps to get that first job:

1. Find jobs online
   a. Indeed (https://www.indeed.com)
   b. Monster (https://www.monster.com)
   c. Glassdoor (https://www.glassdoor.com)
   d. LinkedIn (https://www.linkedin.com)
   e. Believe it or not, Craigslist too—search carefully (https://www.craigslist.org)
2. Find jobs by going to job fairs, also known as career fairs, either at local school campuses or convention centers. You get to talk to many employers all at once, and they have to fight for you as well. Here, time is of the essence.
3. Find jobs through recruiters, especially in a specialized industry if you have a unique skill set. These recruiters are well paid and get anywhere from 25 percent to 100 percent (sometimes more) of your base pay once they succeed in matching you with an employer.
4. Tailor your resume for each job application.
5. Apply for the job.
6. Talk to prospective employers.
7. Interview. Most companies do a combination of phone interviews and several on-site interviews in multiple rounds or with a panel.

8. Learn about the company, its culture and management styles, and its benefits before accepting an offer.

Train, educate yourself or start your own small business now, and start earning now!

I am not going to go into great detail; however, below are a few industries you can look into relatively quickly. With little or no experience and some education—usually a high school diploma or equivalent and/or certification—you can start earning in one of these fields. Just do a basic search online to find the state requirements, schools, and courses, and hit the ground running. These industries include:

1. **Real estate broker**: Basically, you are an agent representing either a buyer of a real estate property or a seller and earning a commission on the deal. This is a great way to earn, as you will have the autonomy of controlling how much you can earn and when you work. Usually you will have to pass a brokerage exam, get certified, and then work under a managing broker, who acts as your general overseer and supervises other agents. You will have to take a course to complete the required hours of broker prelicense coursework and then take and pass the state licensing exam. In the state of Illinois, where I live, ninety hours of broker prelicense coursework are required. The next steps would be for you to activate your license and then become a member of the MLS (Multiple Listing Service) or NAR (National Association of Realtors).

2. **Nursing (CNA):** You can get into this industry by going for a certified nursing assistant (CNA) program. The state-approved training programs are quick to complete—anywhere from three to six months—and will usually include practical training. You will have to pass the certification exam and then get listed on your state's CNA registry.

3. **Nursing (RN):** If you have the funds and time, you can enroll in a nursing program at a college or reputable university. This will lead you down the path to registered nurse (RN). You will have to pass the NCLEX-RN examination and then obtain a state license.

4. **Ride-share driving:** I talked about this in the side hustling section. However, to note it again, once you can get a decent enough car registered in your name and pass the inspection checks for Uber and/or Lyft, you can start driving people around the city in which you live and start making money rather quickly. You will have the flexibility here to set your hours, and this is proportional to your earning capabilities.

5. **Start your own business:** If you have your own skill set, such as tailoring, hairstyling, interior decorating, engineering-related work, or any type of consulting, you can start your own business rather quickly. I would recommend any of the following:

a. Use LegalZoom (https://www.legalzoom.com) for your business formation, be it a sole proprietorship, LLC (limited liability company), or a corporation.

b. You can get your EIN (employer identification number) directly from the US Internal Revenue Service. Visit https://www.IRS.gov.

c. Use websites such as https://legaltemplates.net to get other legal documentation needed for your operating agreements.

d. Do not forget to look into your city and state registration, licenses, and permits. Usually information is available at your local city hall or their website.

e. Get dedicated bank accounts opened for your business, order some business cards, and have a decent online presence on such sites as Twitter, Instagram, or a basic website. Now you are ready to start greeting customers and growing your business.

The bottom line I am trying to convey is, yes, you are relatively new in the United States; however, you are not helpless. There are many industries that could be open to you if you are willing to do the work and start earning right away. Look into this—some of these have legal requirements that are state specific—and start your journey now! Good luck to you!

CHAPTER 7

Taxes

Taxes: Basic definitions

- IRC: Internal revenue code set by the United States Congress. Also known as the Tax Code.
- **IRS**: Internal Revenue Service. Under the US Department of the Treasury, this is an agency dedicated to collecting taxes, auditing and enforcing the rules, and issuing tax refunds, rebates, and credits.
- **Tax refund**: The IRS returns to you what you (the taxpayer) have paid in excess of the actual amount of taxes you owed in the past year.
- **Income taxes**: Taxes imposed directly on income, wages, or salary. The employee is responsible for this. Although the employee is ultimately held legally responsible for paying the taxes, the employer will often withhold an amount from each paycheck and submit the payment to the IRS on behalf of the employee.

- **Payroll taxes**: Tax on the salaries and wages of employees. Both employees and employers contribute to payroll taxes.
- **Sales taxes**: Tax paid by a business to a governing body for the sales of goods and services.
- **Real estate taxes**: Taxes levied on real estate, paid usually to the local governing body.
- **Social Security**: This is a system set up by the US government to assist people with inadequate or no income. Every taxpayer pays into this program.
- **Medicare**: This is a United States national health-insurance program for Americans sixty-five years and up or for people with disability status.
- **Earned income**: Income subject to taxation, including salaries, wages, tips, bonuses, and so on.
- **Unearned income**: Income, also subject to taxation, that includes interest from assets, dividends paid out from shares, profits from the sale of assets, rental income, royalties from intellectual properties, and so on.
- **Tax deductions**: This is the amount by which you, the taxpayer, can reduce the amount of income you will need to pay taxes on. This basically exempts a portion of your income from tax.
- **Tax credits**: This is the amount, dollar for dollar, that you can reduce your tax liability.

- **Social Security number:** This is a number issued to US citizens and residents for the purpose of identification, getting a job, and collecting Social Security benefits and other government services. A nine-digit number is issued to you, and a card with this number is also provided.
- **ITIN:** The individual taxpayer identification number is a tax-processing number for individuals who are required to have US taxpayer identification number but do not have and are not eligible to obtain a Social Security number.
- **EIN:** Employer identification number. Used to identify a business entity. It can be applied for online via the IRS official website, and it is a free service.
- **CPA:** Certified Public Accountant, which is the title given to reputable and qualified accountants in the United States. These accountants are licensed to serve the public accounting services.

Taxes in the United States

Everyone in the United States of America pays taxes. All residents, nonresidents, and US citizens are expected to pay taxes on all worldwide income.

The US tax system is very complex, and it usually changes from year to year how one determines the amount of taxes owed to the government.

What you need to know, as you are new to the United States, is that it is important for you to file your yearly tax returns. Taxes are usually paid for the current year, and one files a tax return for the previous year to determine the amount of a refund or additional payment needed. Tax liabilities are based on the net income of the individual. You can file tax returns under one of the following statuses:

1. Single
2. Married filing separately
3. Married filing jointly
4. Head of household.

It is up to you and your tax accountant or CPA to determine what suits you and your family for the year in which you are filing taxes.

Taxes are of utmost importance, and proof of filing and conformity are usually requested for major deals and investments in the United States—for example, during your immigration process or usually when purchasing assets such as a home.

You have the choice of going to a CPA or tax professional, or you can file your taxes yourself. File electronically or mail it to the IRS.

Taxes for all taxpayers in the United States are due on April 15 if you are a calendar-year filer. An extension can be requested if you cannot file by the due date of your return.

For the most up-to-date information, please visit the official IRS website at https://www.irs.gov/. On this site you will be able to get information on filing taxes, paying taxes, requesting extensions, obtaining relevant forms, and other relevant and critical tax information.

Lastly, you must keep all records of your taxes in whatever format is easiest for you to store. You can also request the transcripts from the IRS directly. Moreover, they now have the capability for you to register and get access to your tax transcript online—usually copies of the last three to five years, depending on the type of transcripts needed.

I personally have physical copies of all my taxes for well over a decade, and I have kept all the documents for proof of income and earnings.

Filing tax returns in the United States

You will not be able to determine for any given year exactly what your tax liability, schedule of tax payments, or refunds for over-payments will be until you figure it out after the year is over. So, tax returns must be filed annually for individuals and businesses with income. Income can be from wages, interest, dividends, and capital gains from the sales of assets or any other profits. Your tax return will be filed with the IRS, and this can be done yourself, or done by CPAs or accounting firms on your behalf, or with online tools from several companies, such as TurboTax and H&R Block. You are usually able to file electronically with the IRS, which takes about three to four weeks to process, or you can mail your taxes and filing documents, which takes about six to eight weeks to process. E-file options include the following:

1. IRS free filing—mostly if your income is less than $66,000 as of the year 2019.

    a. Online taxes at OLT.com: https://www.olt.com/main/oltfree/default.asp

    b. eSmart Free File Edition: https://www.esmart-tax.com/ffa/

    c. 1040NOW.NET: http://www.1040now.net/freefile.htm

    d. TaxAct®Free File: https://www.freetaxact.com/alltax.asp?sc=18050302

    e. 1040.com Free File Edition: https://www.1040.com/IRSFreeFile

    f. H&R Block's Free File: https://www.hrblock. com/ffa/?otpPartnerId=180&campaignId= pw_mcm_180_0001

    g. TaxSlayer: https://www.taxslayer.com/america npledge/?source=TSUSATY2018

    h. Free Tax Returns.com: https://freetaxes. free1040taxreturn.com/

    i. ezTaxReturn.com: https://eztaxreturn.com/ freefilealliance

    j. FileYourTaxes.com: https://www.fileyourtaxes. com/alliance

2. Free tax return preparation sites such as Volunteer Income Tax Assistance (VITA) and Tax Counseling for the Elderly (TCE) programs.

3. Use commercial tax preparation software to prepare and file the taxes. This is then transmitted through IRS-approved electronic channels.

    a. H&R Block (https://www.hrblock.com)

    b. Turbo Tax (https://turbotax.intuit.com)

4. Filing with a tax professional in their office and physical location.

5. Doing it yourself by downloading the needed forms from the IRS official website.

Commonly used IRS tax forms

- Form 1040: Individual Tax Return
- From 1040x: Another version of 1040, for amending a previously filed return
- Form 1040EZ: The simplest version of the 1040, used to file if you have no dependents, are younger than sixty-five, earned less than $100,000, and do not plan to itemize deductions
- Form W-9: Request for Taxpayer Identification Number (TIN) and Certification
- Form 4506-T: Request for Transcript of Tax Return
- Form W-4: Employee's Withholding Allowance Certificate
- Form 941: Employer's Quarterly Federal Tax Return
- Form W-2: Employers engaged in a trade or business who pay compensation
- Form 9465: Installment Agreement Request
- Form 4868: Application for Automatic Extension of Time to File US Individual Income Tax Return
- Form 1099: There are many 1099 forms each, distinguishable by the letters at the end
    a. 1099-B: Reports stock or bond transactions in a brokerage account
    b. 1099-C: Reports canceled debt
    c. 1099-DIV: Reports dividends earned
    d. 1099-INT: Reports interest earned from bank

    e. 1099-G: Reports certain government payments, such as state tax refunds, etc.

    f. 1099-MISC: Reports miscellaneous income

    g. 1099-R: Reports pension or annuity income or IRA distributions

    h. 1099-Q: Reports distributions from qualified tuition programs

    i. 1099-S: Reports proceeds from the sale or swap of real estate properties

    j. 1099-SA: Reports distribution from health savings accounts and the like

    k. SSA-1099: Reports income from Social Security

- Form 1098: This is the mortgage interest statement, which reports the amount of interest paid.

- Form 1098-E: This is the student loan interest statement, which reports the amount of loan interest the recipient paid during the year.

- Form 1098-T: This is a statement that reports the amount of tuition and fees received by a qualified educational institution.

- Form 1095-A: This is the form the health-insurance marketplace sends you if you bought your health insurance through it.

- Form 1095-B: This form from your health-insurance company shows who is covered and the duration of coverage. It is for those individuals and members of their family who had health coverage that is not reported on the 1095-A or 1095-C form.

- Form 1095-C: This is a form showing the individuals who are covered by the employer's health coverage and the duration of coverage.

- Schedule C: This is the P/L (profit and loss) statement for reporting to the IRS from a business that is part of the individual's income tax return.

CHAPTER 8

Immigration

Immigration, United States

American immigration is super complex, and it's one of the most divisive issues and topics in the land. It comes up almost every election cycle, and there are always multiple opposing sides and views.

Your immigration status in the United States of America must always be front and center, and you must have an understanding of where you are and where you would like to go or be. There are basically two final destinations regarding your immigration status. Quite frankly, maybe even only one; the first one can lead to the second. These are:

1. Green card, officially known as the primary resident card.

2. United States citizenship.

Some of you reading this book or chapter are likely either on a visiting/tourist visa, student visa, medical tourism visa, or temporary employment visa, or you have a status such as the OPT (optional practical training), the H1B visa, and so on. What you should know is that all these statuses and visas are temporary—they do expire, requiring you to return to your home country.

If America is the place you want to be, establish your presence, have a family, and live a prosperous new life, you must take this matter very seriously. Seek professional legal advice and help, and always stay up to date with the current laws.

One thing you should note: it is critical for you to live a life free of crime. Do not break any laws, and always be forthcoming and honest as you deal with the US government. Any issues, lies, omissions, or nondisclosures...well, would significantly complicate your situation.

There are several reasons for you to want to come to the United States of America: tourism, business, employment, study, or immigration. My intention in this chapter is not to exhaust all the possibilities of the American immigration laws and systems; however, after this chapter you should be able to start asking the right questions and seek the best legal expertise to intervene on your behalf.

You can start the immigration process to the United States whether you are residing abroad via an immigrant visa application or are already residing in the United States under another visa category, at which point you would initiate the adjustment of status process.

Enjoy reading, and good luck.

Immigration: common terms

USCIS: United States Customs and Immigration Service

NVC: National Visa Center

CBP: Customs and Border Protection, also known as USCBP

ICE: Immigration and Customs Enforcement

DHS: Department of Homeland Security, the agency of the federal government responsible for the security of the homeland—pretty much the security of the United States of America. USCIS, CBP, and ICE all are subagencies of the DHS.

LPR: Lawful permanent resident. This is the immigration status given to anyone who has been approved via the necessary submittal of forms and evidence to indefinitely stay, live, and work in the United States.

AOS: Adjustment of status is the term used when you apply for your green card to become a lawful permanent resident.

Green Card: A common name used for the card issued by the government as evidence of lawful permanent residence.

1-94 Arrival/Departure Record: Issued to you at the port of entry, by CBP, as evidence of your arrival and departure from the United States of America. It usually will contain information on dates, length of stay approved, type of visa, and any conditions of stay.

Naturalization: This is the process by which a non–US citizen or LPR qualifies and has met all the necessary requirements to apply and become a citizen of the United States of America. This is usually dependent on the conditions of LPR and length of continuous and physical presence in the USA.

Visa: Well, you should know this one. If you don't know…hmm. In the spirit of information, this is a document issued to anyone as a permit to present to the CBP at the port of entry to gain entry into the United States. Many other countries also issue visas for the same purposes. Note that a visa is not a guarantee of entering the United States. This is usually stamped or fixed into your passport.

The immigrant visa process

Foreign citizens who wish to have a permanent life in the United States of America must first obtain an immigrant visa. This is the first step and cannot be avoided.

This is from the travel.state.gov website:

> Immigrating to the United States is an important and complex decision. In this section, you will learn about who may immigrate to the United States, the different types of immigrant visas, the required forms, and the steps in the immigrant visa process. Because most immigrants receive visas in the family or employment based visa categories, they are a key focus of this section. To be eligible to apply for an immigrant visa, a foreign citizen must be sponsored by a US citizen relative, US lawful permanent resident, or a prospective employer, with a few exceptions, explained below. The sponsor begins the immigration process by filing a petition on the foreign citizen's behalf with US Citizenship and Immigration Services (USCIS).[6]

6 "Homepage." USCIS, www.uscis.gov/.

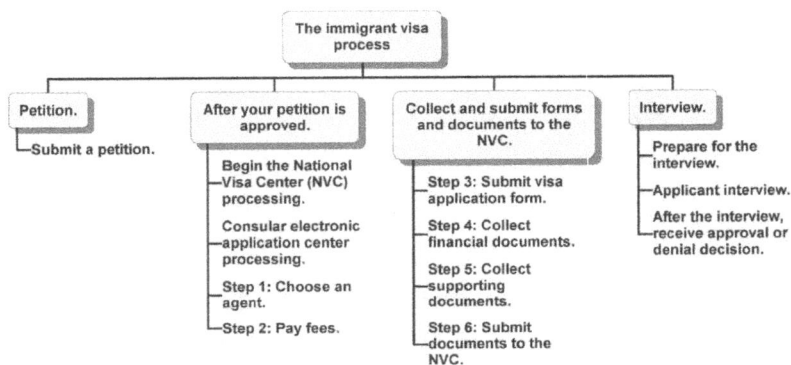

Note: Usually, someone else must file the petition for you, usually a US citizen or a lawful permanent resident.

Sources: https://travel.state.gov, https://www.uscis.gov/greencard?tabshow=1

Flow chart: green card eligibility

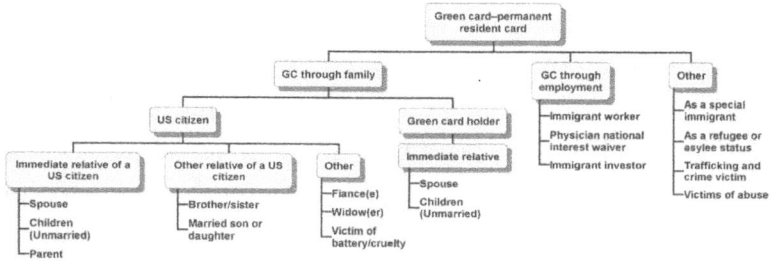

The above is a flowchart showing the different paths one can take in applying or obtaining a green card. You must choose what fits your situation, know the requirements, and seek expert help to facilitate.

Websites:

- https://www.uscis.gov/greencard
- https://www.uscis.gov/greencard/eligibility-categories
- https://www.uscis.gov/greencard?tabshow=1

Please visit the sites named above, read them, and study them. They will help you gain the necessary understanding of current laws, their requirements, and the process you will need to follow. Are you eligible to apply? Are you inside or outside the United States? These questions will be answered as you begin this journey.

United States citizenship

Obtaining United States citizenship is complex and requires a lot of proof and evidence, and certain requirements must be met. From the chart below, citizenship can be obtained either at birth or after birth. Note that naturalization is an option for you if you went through the adjustment of status, became a lawful permanent resident, and have fulfilled certain requirements.

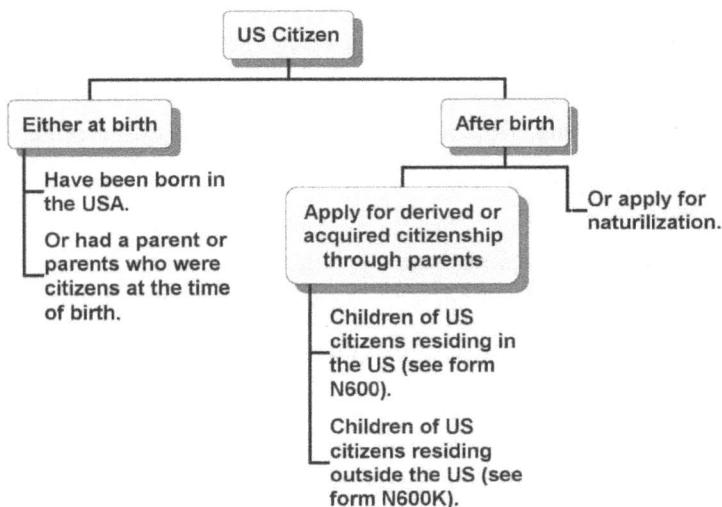

Websites:

- https://www.uscis.gov/us-citizenship
- https://www.uscis.gov/us-citizenship/citizenship-through-parents
- https://www.uscis.gov/us-citizenship/citizenship-through-naturalization

Employment authorization (work permit):

Depending on what your status is and the current applications you have in process, the US government understands the need to work and earn so you can survive and support yourself and your family. Hence, you may seek employment authorization, applied for by filing form I-765. Once it's approved, an employment authorization document (EAD) card is issued and is proof that the holder is able to work legally in the United States.

Form I-765 can be applied for under several categories. To name a few:

1. Asylee/refugee (and their spouses and children)
2. Nationality categories such as citizen of Micronesia; temporary protected status (TPS)
3. Foreign student categories such as:
    a. F1 students seeking optional practical training (OPT) in a position directly related to their major area of study
    b. Twenty-four-month extension for STEM (science, technology, engineering, and math) students. Usually this can be applied for up to ninety days before the expiration of your OPT.
    c. F1 student seeking off-campus employment due to severe economic hardship
4. Diplomatic missions, international organizations, or NATO

5. Employment-based nonimmigrant categories:
   a. Spouse of L-1 intracompany transferee
   b. Spouse of an H-1B nonimmigrant
6. Family-based nonimmigrant categories:
   a. K-1 nonimmigrant fiancé(e) of us citizen or K-2 dependent
   b. K-3 nonimmigrant spouse of us citizen or K-4 dependent
7. Adjustment of status categories
8. Adjustment applicant

There are many more categories not mentioned. However, you should know that most likely, while you are in the United States, there is a great chance that you can gain employment authorization under the correct category. The US government understands the need to earn and provide for your family, so to continue your education, please visit this website: https://www.uscis.gov/i-765.

H1-B program

The H1-B is a program administered by the US government. It allows companies based in the United States the opportunity to hire foreign workers, usually those who possess a required skill, talent, or expertise that is not easily or readily available in the current employee pool. The program typically issues a visa to those who have applied and are approved. This is called the H1-B visa. This is a nonimmigrant visa, and it is usually good for three years with an option to renew.

There are only a certain number of visas available to those who have applied to this program. The US government usually has a cap on the number of visas granted per year. A certain portion of the visas is reserved for those who hold advanced and higher degrees such as master's and PhD degrees in fields such as science, engineering, and information technology.

Applicants usually must hold a bachelor's degree or higher, and applications must be filed no more than six months before the employment start date requested for the beneficiary.

Form I-129, the petition for a nonimmigrant worker, is used. Please note: individuals cannot apply directly for the H1-B. The employer must petition for them.

Websites:
- https://www.uscis.gov/i-129
- https://www.uscis.gov/working-united-states/tempo-rary-workers/h-1b-specialty-occupations-and-fashion-models/h-1b-fiscal-year-fy-2020-cap-season

Other visas worth mentioning for your information and research:

- L-1B for specialized workers
- L-1A for managers and executives
- E-2 Treaty investor visa
- E-1 Treaty trader visa; E-3 for Australians

Most popular immigration forms

From the US government website (https://www.uscis.gov/forms), below are some of the most popular immigration forms used. You can check them out for yourself on the site to get a better understanding.

1. Apply for Citizenship (Form N-400)
2. Apply for a Green Card (Form I-485)
3. Petition for Alien Relative (Form I-130)
4. Apply for Employment Authorization (Form I-765)
5. Affidavit of Support (Form I-864)
6. Employment Eligibility Verification (Form I-9)
7. Apply for a Travel Document (Form I-131)
8. Remove Conditions on a Green Card through Marriage (Form I-751)
9. Renew or Replace My Green Card (Form I-90)
10. G-1055, Fee Schedule

Always go to the uscis.gov website to get the latest document and ensure you have the correct version or edition. The laws change often, fees change often, and it is up to you to ensure you are informed. If you're using legal experts to aid your case, I would advise you follow them every step of the way and never use a hands-off approach to your case.

How to bring your partner or spouse to the USA

There are basically four ways to bring your partner or spouse to the United States of America. These include the following:

1. The K1 visa. The K1 visa is also commonly known as the fiancé visa. This is the visa issued to the fiancé of a lawful permanent resident or the fiancé of a US citizen for the exclusive purpose of coming to the US and marrying within ninety days of admittance into the country.

2. This visa is very useful for those who do not want to be apart from their spouse after marriage. The process usually takes anywhere from eight to ten months. It costs about $1,140 in filing fees.

3. The K3 visa: I won't talk much about this, as it's slowly becoming obsolete and being phased out. This is a visa issued to the spouse of an LPR or the spouse of a US citizen to gain admittance into the United States, for the exclusive purpose of waiting for the approval of an immigrant petition. So, to put it simply, it's a visa for your spouse to come to the US to wait for his or her green card.

4. The CR1/IR1 visa: This is the visa issued after an immigrant petition has been filed and approved by an LPR or a US citizen to gain admittance into the United States. After you enter the US, your green card will be mailed to you here. This usually takes

anywhere from fourteen to eighteen months. It costs about $1,540.

5. If you and your spouse have been married for less than two years after the issuance of the visa, it will be a CR1 visa. If the visa is issued after you have celebrated your two-year anniversary, then it will be an IR1 visa.

6. If your spouse is already in the United States, then all that is needed, assuming that you are an LPR or a US citizen, is to apply for adjustment of status.

Flowchart: How to bring your partner or spouse to the United States

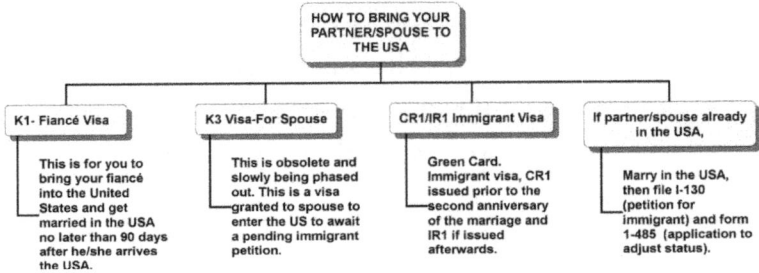

HOW TO BRING YOUR PARTNER/SPOUSE TO THE USA			
K1- Fiancé Visa	**K3 Visa-For Spouse**	**CR1/IR1 Immigrant Visa**	**If partner/spouse already in the USA,**
This is for you to bring your fiancé into the United States and get married in the USA no later than 90 days after he/she arrives the USA.	This is obsolete and slowly being phased out. This is a visa granted to spouse to enter the US to await a pending immigrant petition.	Green Card. Immigrant visa, CR1 issued prior to the second anniversary of the marriage and IR1 if issued afterwards.	Marry in the USA, then file I-130 (petition for immigrant) and form I-485 (application to adjust status).

The flowchart above shows the four most commonly used methods to bring your spouse or partner to the United States. We will discuss in detail the K1 visa process and the CR1/IR1 immigrant visa process.

Bring your fiancé/partner using the K1 visa

The K1 visa is also commonly known as the fiancé visa.

Process:

1. LPR or US citizen files I-129F with the USCIS. If approved, it goes to the NVC.
2. After NVC clerical processing, the fiancé(e) applies for a K1 visa at a US consulate abroad.

Key information:

3. This is for your fiancé, which means you and he/she must be engaged. You both must be available to marry, you must have a legitimate relationship, and you must have met in person within the past two years.
4. This usually takes about eight to ten months from application to approval, barring no issues or requests for evidence (RFEs). RFEs usually delay most applications to the USCIS.
5. The form used is the I-129F, petition for alien fiancé(e)
6. It is a single-entry visa issued for the exclusive purpose of marrying within ninety days of arrival to the US. This visa is usually valid for six months. After admittance into the US and marriage within ninety days, you must apply for a green card.

7. This whole process, including the application for green card, usually costs about $2,465. Note: please always check the USCIS websites for the current forms and filing fees.

8. Dependent children can be included at the time of the application. This is a K2 visa—a dependent visa.

9. You must be truthful in all applications and in any representation of yourself and your marriage. Some red flags that could make your case end in a denial are the following:

   o There is a large age gap between you and your fiancé(e)

   o You have never met your partner.

   o No one—family or friends—knows the person or that you are getting married.

   o You do not speak a common language.

   o Your statements do not match each other's, or there are inconsistencies in your stories.

   o You have previously filed immigration petitions.

Flowchart: Bring your fiancé/partner to the US using the K1 visa

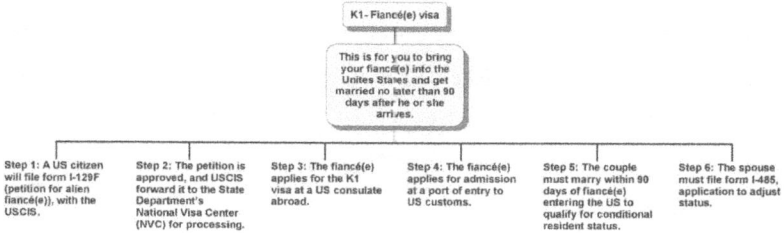

K1 - Fiancé(e) visa

This is for you to bring your fiancé(e) into the Unites States and get married no later than 90 days after he or she arrives.

Step 1: A US citizen will file form I-129F (petition for alien fiancé(e)), with the USCIS.

Step 2: The petition is approved, and USCIS forward it to the State Department's National Visa Center (NVC) for processing.

Step 3: The fiancé(e) applies for the K1 visa at a US consulate abroad.

Step 4: The fiancé(e) applies for admission at a port of entry to US customs.

Step 5: The couple must marry within 90 days of fiancé(e) entering the US to qualify for conditional resident status.

Step 6: The spouse must file form I-485, application to adjust status.

The flowchart above shows the steps and process for applying for the K1 visa. As you can see, once you have gained admittance into the United States and gotten married within ninety days, you must proceed to file an application to adjust your status.

CR1/IR1—green card for your spouse

This is the visa issued after an immigrant petition has been filed and approved by an LPR or a US citizen to gain admittance into the United States. After you enter the country, your green card will be mailed to you here. This usually takes anywhere from fourteen to eighteen months.

Process:

- An LPR or US citizen files an I-130 form, the petition for an alien relative, with the USCIS.
- Once this is approved, it is sent to the NVC for clerical processing, at which point more documents and information are gathered.
- This approved petition is then sent to the US embassy in the foreign country, at which point the alien relative passes a medical examination and must go through the interview. Once approved, an immigrant visa is issued, and it is presented along with relevant documents by the alien relative at the port of entry to CBP to gain admittance.
- After admittance into the United States, the green card is sent in the mail to your spouse, and he or she is now a lawful permanent resident (LPR).

Key information:

- It is for your spouse, which means you must be married.
- This usually takes about fourteen to eighteen months, from application to approval, barring any issues or requests for evidence (RFEs). RFEs usually delay applications to the USCIS. RFEs are issued for a number of reasons, such as insufficient evidence to support the application, incomplete applications, and misrepresentation.
- The form used is the I-130, the petition for alien relative, filed by the LPR or US citizen.
- A CR1 spousal visa is issued if the marriage is less than two years old. If it's older than two years, an IR1 visa is issued.
- This whole process, including the application for the green card, usually costs about $1,540. Note: please always check the USCIS website for the current forms and filing fees.
- Dependent children can be included at the time of the application. However, a separate application is needed for each dependent at the time of filing, with a separate filing fee for each.
- You must be truthful in all applications and in any representation of yourself and your marriage. Some red flags that could make your case end in a denial are the following:

o   There is a large age gap between you and your fiancé(e)

o   You have never met your partner.

o   No one—family or friends—knows the person or that you are getting married.

o   You do not speak a common language.

o   Your statements do not match each other's, or there are inconsistencies in your stories.

o   You have previously filed immigration petitions.

Flowchart: CR1/IR1, green card for your spouse

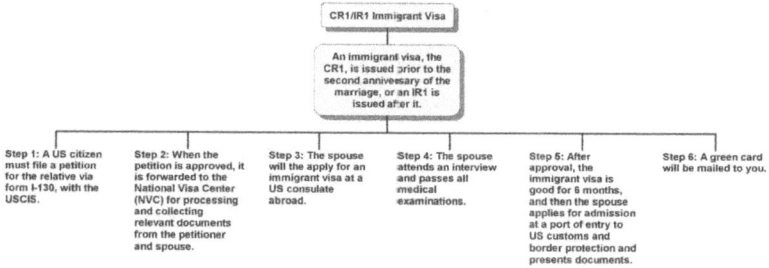

CR1/IR1 Immigrant Visa

An immigrant visa, the CR1, is issued prior to the second anniversary of the marriage, or an IR1 is issued after it.

Step 1: A US citizen must file a petition for the relative via form I-130, with the USCIS.	Step 2: When the petition is approved, it is forwarded to the National Visa Center (NVC) for processing and collecting relevant documents from the petitioner and spouse.	Step 3: The spouse will the apply for an immigrant visa at a US consulate abroad.	Step 4: The spouse attends an interview and passes all medical examinations.	Step 5: After approval, the immigrant visa is good for 6 months, and then the spouse applies for admission at a port of entry to US customs and border protection and presents documents.	Step 6: A green card will be mailed to you.

The flowchart above shows the steps and process for applying for your spouse's immigrant visa. Once an approved petition is completed and the alien relative (spouse) goes through the interview and medical exam and then gains entry to the United States, the green card is sent via mail to you and your spouse.

CHAPTER 9

Sex Culture

Notable definitions

- **Heterosexuality**: This is attraction to or sexual involvement with people of the opposite sex.
- **Bisexuality**: Attraction to or engagement in sexual relations with people of both the male and female genders.
- **Gay**: Being attracted to or engaging in sexual activities with someone of the same gender.
- **Lesbian**: A female who is attracted to other females.
- **Transgender**: People who do not identify with the sex of their genitalia and feel they belong to the opposite sex—for example, a person with a penis who identifies as and feels like a woman.
- **Gender nonbinary**: People who don't feel they belong to either the male or female sex, irrespective of the genitals they were born with.
- **Allosexual**: Those who experience sexual desires.

- **Asexual**: Those who experience no sexual desires.
- **Sexual consent**: Permission for something to happen or agreement to do something related to sexual activity. Without consent, it is rape.
- **Age of consent**: This is the age required to legally consent to sexual behavior.
- **Statutory rape**: Nonforcible sexual activity in which one of the individuals is below the age of consent.
- **Stealthing**: I thought it prudent to include this, as I just found out the meaning myself. This is a practice in which a man stealthily removes or damages his condom during intercourse without his partner's knowledge or consent, when the partner has only given consent to condom-protected sex. This is very wrong. It is unacceptable, and criminal charges could be brought against you.
- **Morning-after pill**: Also known as Plan B, this is a pill now available over the counter to be used in the event of an emergency—for example, after having unprotected sex or in the event of failure of other contraceptives or birth control.
- **STDs/STIs**: Sexually transmitted disease/infection. This is an infection transmitted through sexual contact, caused by bacteria, viruses, or parasites. Common ones are genital herpes, chlamydia, human papillomavirus infection, HIV/AIDS, gonorrhea, and syphilis, just to name a few.

Consent

Again, let me welcome you to the United States of America, the land of plenty. One of the things you will quickly learn is the diversity of the sex culture in America.

A big topic of discussion—and one we should all understand—is the need for and the importance of consent in any sexual engagement.

Simply put, a NO = NO = NO!

Please be very mindful and always conduct yourself in a responsible and respectful manner. The consequences otherwise are very serious and will spell the end of your career here in the United States before it even begins—and oh, did I mention jail time? Yes, jail time.

As a young fellow, you came here in pursuit of your dreams, maybe to study, to do well for yourself and make your family proud. Let this page be a note of caution to you. Key points:

- When your partner says no, please stop the encounter. There are no buts here.
- Do not participate in any sexual encounters with anyone under the influence of drugs and/or alcohol.
- As a young woman, always employ the buddy system when on campus, when it's late or dark, and when you're walking to your home, dorm, car, or to/from work or a night out with friends.

- Remember, always gain consent. I cannot say this enough: NO means NO!

Contraceptives, part I—birth control

There are many options for contraceptives and birth control available to you in America. These can prevent sexually transmitted diseases and/or unwanted pregnancies. The table below highlights a few of them:

Contraceptive	Detail	Effective Rate
Condoms	This is the only contraceptive that helps prevent both STDs and pregnancy.	87 percent
IUD	This is a T-shaped device that is placed inside the uterus to prevent pregnancy. IUD stands for intrauterine device.	99 percent
Injection/Shot	An injection of the hormone progestin is given to the woman in the buttocks or arm.	96 percent
The pill / combined oral contraceptive	A prescribed pill containing estrogen and progestin. It is taken at the same time every day.	93 percent
Patch	A skin patch worn on the arm or abdomen to release the hormones progestin and estrogen into the bloodstream.	93 percent

Ring	This is placed inside the vagina to release hormones.	93 percent
Diaphragm / cervical cap	This is placed inside the vagina to cover the cervix, thereby blocking the entry of sperm.	83 percent
Female condom	This is worn by the woman to help keep the sperm from getting into her body.	79 percent

Contraceptives, part II

Please consult with your family doctor for information and advice regarding your health-care plan. The table below details the other two forms of contraceptives, the emergency ones and the permanent ones for both men and women.

Contraceptive	Detail	Effective Rate
Emergency	This is typically to be used with 72 hours of unprotected sex. These usually are known as morning-after pills, used after sex to stop a pregnancy before it starts. Common brands include Next Choice, My Way, Plan B One-Step, and Take Action. Most of them do not need a prescription and are available at a drug or convenience store.	85–90 percent

| Permanent | Both men and women have the choice here. These are sterilization methods used to prevent pregnancies permanently. The procedure for men is a vasectomy, and for women, it is a tubal ligation.

Vasectomy: The tube that carries the sperm, called the vas deferens, is cut and tied. The process is usually reversible.

Tubal ligation: Both of the fallopian tubes in a woman are closed so the sperm cannot get to the egg. | 99 percent |

Abortion and abortion rights

Let us start with the simple fact: ABORTION IS LEGAL IN THE UNITED STATES.

Now let's continue. According to Wikipedia, "Abortion is among the most controversial and divisive issues in the society, culture and politics of the United States." In 1973, the Supreme Court of the United States, in the case of Roe v. Wade, legalized abortion nationwide.[7]

Various states in recent times have been either actively or passively trying to chip away at this law or restrict it in one form or the other. So, you need to know the states and their laws, specifically the latest point in pregnancy when a woman can get an abortion—for example, no limit or thirteen weeks. These are the two extremes until some states ban abortion outright, which as of 2019 is yet to happen.

Two main opposing views of abortion exist in mainstream America. From the Planned Parenthood website, they are as follows:

1. **Pro-choice:** People who believe that women have the basic human right to decide when and whether to have children, based on their own moral and religious beliefs, even though they themselves may not choose abortion as an option for unplanned pregnancies.

---

7 "Abortion in the United States," *Wikipedia*, Wikimedia Foundation, January 22, 2020, en.wikipedia.org/wiki/Abortion_in_the_United_States.

2. **Pro-life:** People who oppose abortion. Many of them do not believe that a woman should be able to choose abortion under any circumstances, even if she has been raped or if carrying the pregnancy to term puts her life in danger.

An interesting fact I just came across—I really didn't know this—is that one in every four pregnancies will end naturally due to being a nonviable pregnancy—a miscarriage.

Same-sex marriage and LGBTQ

Regardless of what is actually legal or morally correct, there are people who are not tolerant of behaviors that are not exclusively heterosexual, and sometimes those people can be openly hostile.

Most importantly, I want to use this section to let you know that same-sex marriage has been ruled legal by the highest court in the United States, the Supreme Court, since 2015. For years, couples of the same sex couldn't enjoy the benefits and protections offered by the institution of marriage. You should know that even though the practice is legal, like abortion rights, this ruling is always under attack, mostly from conservative groups and some religious groups.

I would like you to research the following topics as you expand your own knowledge:

- Lesbian, gay, bisexual, transgender, and queer (LGBTQ)
- What does *queer* mean?
- What does it mean to be transgender?
- What is gender expression?
- What does *questioning* mean?
- What is gender identity?
- What does cisgender mean?
- What are the issues and concerns facing the LGBTQ community at home, school, the office, and so on?

As you encounter the many and different communities in America, irrespective of your personal choices and beliefs, they must be respected and treated like any other citizens in the United States, free from prejudice. Same-sex marriage is usually associated with the LGBTQ community. LGBTQ stands for lesbian, gay, bisexual, transgender, and queer or questioning.

Well done! You have just finished reading this book, and I know you are optimistic and confident in your new found home, America. Let your creative juices flow and your thoughts be stimulated. I want to encourage you to continue to unlock your potential every day, and remember that the best time to start anything was yesterday, the next best time is today. Ask the right questions that are critical to your success, make a robust plan, and always back it up with purposeful action.

I want to thank you, sincerely, for the time you have taken out of your busy lives to read this book, and spending time with me. You are a rock star! I wish you the very best of luck, and many great opportunities to come your way.

To get more useful information, join us at www.verticalos. com. You will find many useful offerings, including e-courses, workshops, useful templates for you, and bonus content. I'd also love to hear from you all. Get a hold of me via twitter @ VerticalOS or email me at Michael@verticalos.com (Yes this is my actual email).

ACKNOWLEDGMENTS

I want to thank the following:

First of all, the Almighty God, for everything he has done in my life, the blessings he has bestowed upon me, and the thought, the wisdom, and the courage to pursue and complete this book.

My mother, Abosede Abidoye, the woman who is strength personified, my teacher who always supported me in all ways. I thank you sincerely from the bottom of my heart for your love, kindness, and compassion toward me and others.

My father, Captain Olugbemiga Abidoye, the man I most adore, for whom I have the greatest love and respect, who is the biggest cheerleader for his children, for his ever-present love, guidance, and support. I thank you so much, Dad.

My wonderful family, Olaitan, Tunde, Segun, Biodun, Tosin, and Seun, who always encourage me to keep pushing hard and be better. For your support throughout the journey of this book, your insights, role playing, and your counsel on early drafts, I am most thankful.

Imelda, for sharing your life with me and teaching me so much, of which only a fraction is captured in here. For your love and support over so many years, without which this book would never have materialized, I am eternally grateful.

Desmond and Veronica, for your support over the many years we have known each other. Your strategic input, involvement, and contributions were vital in the completion of this book. I thank you so much. Desmond, give me platinum or give me nothing.

Waliy, for the many nights of deliberations and discussions—they sure came in very handy. Thank you for sticking with me through many debates that played vital roles in the formulation of key concepts in this book.

Caprice, for your constant encouragement, support, love, and positivity—I could always count on them. For the many interviews and key contributions, I am sincerely thankful.

Everyone on my editing and publishing team, the Elite Authors team, thank you for helping me on this incredible journey toward getting this book out there. Special thanks to Jenny and Lydia, who were always there helping me navigate unfamiliar territories, for their endless patience with me.

Omo A, Dr. Josef, a special thanks to you all for your many contributions throughout the different phases in the life cycle of the book.

Pat, Chaz, William, Alisa, Theeb, and Colleen, great leaders who have encouraged, coached, and mentored me throughout the years, both personally and professionally. I sincerely thank you.

ACKNOWLEDGMENTS

My early readers and members of VerticalOS. A big thank you for your support, your feedback, and the privilege for letting me play a small part in your journey toward a better life for you and those in your lives.

Everyone who knowingly or unknowingly shared lessons and wisdom and taught me something. I am forever grateful.

WORKS CITED

"American Culture: Study in the USA." *International Student.*
www.internationalstudent.com/study_usa/way-of-life/
american-culture/.

"Birth Control." Wikipedia. Wikimedia Foundation,
November 1, 2019. http://en.wikipedia.org/wiki/
Birth_control.

"Contraception." Centers for Disease Control and Prevention.
November 1, 2019. www.cdc.gov/reproductivehealth/con-
traception/index.htm.

Corlis, Nick. "Difference between Protection, Birth Control,
& Contraception." *STD Exposed—Sexual Health Blog,*
March 4, 2019. http://www.stdcheck.com/blog/difference-
between-protection-birth-control-and-contraception/.

"Credit Karma." Credit Karma. http://www.creditkarma.
com/.

"Credit Report Basics." Experian, August 24, 2019. http://
www.experian.com/blogs/ask-experian/credit-education/
report-basics/.

"Credit Report Information: Guide to Credit Reports."
Equifax. http://www.equifax.com/personal/education/
credit/ report/.

"Credit Score in the United States." Wikipedia. Wikimedia
Foundation. November 12, 2019. http://en.wikipedia.org/
wiki/Credit_score_in_the_United_States.

"Credit Score Information: Guide to Credit Scores." Equifax.
http://www.equifax.com/personal/education/credit/score/.

"Culture Shock." Wikipedia. Wikimedia Foundation.
November 6, 2019. en.wikipedia.org/wiki/Culture_shock.

"Culture Shock: Study in the USA." *International Student.*
http://www.internationalstudent.com/study_usa/way-of-
life/ culture-shock/.

"Daylight Saving Time in the United States."
Wikipedia. Wikimedia Foundation. November
21, 2019. http://en.wikipedia.org/wiki/
Daylight_saving_time_in_the_United_States.

Denning, Tim. "How to Improve Yourself in the Next 6
Months with Very Little Effort." The Ascent. Medium.
September 21, 2018. http://medium.com/the-ascent/how-
to-improve-yourself-in-the-next-6-months-with-very-little-
effort-14117d54bfcd.

Devaney, Tim, et al. "How to Improve Your Credit Health."
Credit Karma. August 12, 2019. http://www.creditkarma.
com/ advice/i/quick-tips-build-credit/.

"Education in the United States of America." WENR. April 16, 2019. http://wenr.wes.org/2018/06/ education-in-the-united-states-of-america.

"Finding Health Insurance." USA.gov. http://www.usa.gov/ finding-health-insurance.

"5k Training." MarathRookie.com. http://www.marathon-rookie.com/5k-training.html.

"Home Page." Annual Credit Report. http://www.annualcreditreport.com/index.action.

"Home Page." Internal Revenue Service. http://www.irs.gov/.

"Home Page." USCIS, www.uscis.gov/.

"How to Build Credit." Experian. October 11, 2019. http:// www. experian.com/blogs/ask-experian/credit-education/ improving-credit/building-credit/.

"International Credential Evaluation." World Education Services. http://www.wes.org/?gclid=EAIaIQobChMI hsntvNns5QIVxIVaBR3MXQKPEAAYAyAAEgLmy _D_BwE.

"Investing: Personalized Investment Advice." Betterment. http://www.betterment.com/investing/.

Issa, Erin El, et al. "How to Build Credit." NerdWallet. July 8, 2019. http://www.nerdwallet.com/blog/finance/ how-to-build-credit/?trk=nw_gn1_4.0.

Kiyosaki, Robert T., and Sharon L. Lechter. *Rich Dad Poor Dad: What the Rich Teach Their Kids about Money-That the Poor and Middle Class Do Not!* Warner, 2000.

"Money Matters: Study in the USA." International Student. http://www.internationalstudent.com/study_usa/way-of-life/ money-matters/.

O'Shea, Bev, et al. "Credit Score Ranges: How Do You Compare?" NerdWallet. September 13, 2019. http://www.nerdwallet.com/blog/finance/ credit-score-ranges-and-how-to-improve/?trk=nw_gn1_4.0.

"Politics of the United States." Wikipedia. Wikimedia Foundation. November 12, 2019. http://en.wikipedia.org/ wiki/Politics_of_the_United_States.

"The Power of International Education." IIE. http://www.iie. org/.

Raynier, Linda. "Stand Out & Get Hired 1:1 Career Coaching Program—Linda Raynier: Career Strategist: Career Coach." Linda Raynier. http://www.lindaraynier. com/standoutgethired.

———. "Who Is Linda Raynier? My Story & What I Do." YouTube. http://www.youtube.com/ watch?v=AZSOwikZ8Rk.

Sabatier, Grant, and Vicki Robin. *Financial Freedom: A Proven Path to All the Money You Will Ever Need.* Avery, 2019.

St. John, Richard. "8 Secrets of Success." TED. http:// www.ted.com/talks/richard_st_john_s_8_secrets_of_ success?language=en#t-185863.

————. *The 8 Traits Successful People Have in Common: 8 to Be Great*. Train of Thought Arts, 2010.

"The Service." Fundrise. http://fundrise.com/investing-with-fundrise?cta=Main%2BMenu.

"7 Things That Won't Hurt Your Credit Scores." Equifax. July 23, 2019. http://www. equifax.com/personal/education/credit/score/7-things-that-wont-hurt-credit-scores/.

"Sexual Consent." Wikipedia. Wikimedia Foundation, November 8, 2019. http://en.wikipedia.org/wiki/Sexual_consent.

Shen, Kristy, and Bryce Leung. *Quit like a Millionaire: No Gimmicks, Luck, or Trust Fund Required*. TarcherPerigee, 2019.

"Social Security." United States Social Security Administration. http://www.ssa.gov/.

"STEM." STEM—Biocom Life Science Association of California. http://www.biocom.org/what-we-offer/biocom-institute/stem/.

"Uber Eats." Uber Eats. http://www.ubereats.com/en-US/restaurants-near-me/.

"United States." Wikipedia. Wikimedia Foundation. November 12, 2019. http://en.wikipedia.org/wiki/United_States.

"What Affects Your Credit Scores?" Experian. March 11, 2019. http://www.experian.com/

blogs/ask-experian/credit-education/ score-basics/
what-affects-your-credit-scores/.
"What Are the Different Credit Score Ranges?"
Experian. September 16, 2019. http://
www.experian.com/blogs/ask-experian/
infographic-what-are-the-different-scoring-ranges/.
"What Is a Credit Score & How Is It Affected?" TransUnion.
http://www.transunion.com/credit-score.
"What Key Factors Impact My Credit Scores?" Credit Karma
Help Center. http://help.creditkarma.com/hc/en-us/
articles/203484364-What-key-factors-impact-my-cred-
itscores.
White, Jennifer. "Who Can Help Me Build My Credit?"
Experian. November 14, 2019. http://www.experian.com/
blogs/ask-experian/who-can-help-me-build-my-credit/.

Olusegun Abidoye is the founder of VerticalOS.com. Born and raised in Lagos, Nigeria, Abidoye immigrated to the United States to pursue higher education, earning a master of science in electrical engineering and specializing in controls and embedded systems. He has worked for several Fortune 500 companies, including Nestlé, Archer Daniels Midland, and Crown Cork & Seal. Abidoye now dedicates VerticalOS to providing content and consulting services to everyday people to improve their lives wherever they may be.

www.ingramcontent.com/pod-product-compliance
Lightning Source LLC
Chambersburg PA
CBHW021100090426
42738CB00006B/433